# Revitalizing Real Madrid

## The Tactics and Stats behind Zinedine Zidane's Success

## Scott Martin

To my wife, Melissa, and our two boys, Sammy and Joe.

I love you and am blessed to have you in my life.

# Contents

# Introduction

Tactics have always fascinated me.

Maybe that's because I was a slow-footed #6 in a 1-4-4-2 diamond midfield with two wide midfielders. To shut down the opposition's midfield, I had to think a couple of steps in advance to be effective. My pace couldn't do the job, so my mind had to take control.

It could also just be my love for systems, be it on the soccer field (sorry non-American crowd) or elsewhere. Graduate studies in philosophy and theology offered so much enjoyment. Following the history of thought in Western Civilization, starting with one of my favorite philosophers, Aristotle, and leading to John Searle's philosophy of the mind courses at UC Berkeley, grad school was a time and place to develop my understanding of systems of thought and understanding the nature of responses.

It's during that time I started coaching at a local high school. A good friend mentioned her school needed a coach for the girls' program, so I snapped up the opportunity. Club coaching followed, as did collegiate work at Belmont Abbey College in North Carolina.

My approach to coaching followed the same feverish pattern as my graduate studies. Never content with what I knew, I used my team's performances as a compass for study. Wherever we struggled, that issue became the focus of my studies.

While coaching in Northern California, personal development came in a nice package. The association brought in the like of Frans Hoek (then the Dutch national team assistant coach) and Vincenzo Vergine (Fiorentina's academy manager), as well as coaches from Europe's top academies, such as Benfica, Ajax, Tottenham, PSV, and Motherwell.

It was a youth coach's dream come true.

Moving across the country, those opportunities vanished. While losing that access was certainly a negative, it forced me to take control of my coaching development.

The team-led study continued, as did my awareness of websites like Spielverlagerung and The Coaches' Voice.

Back in March 2019, while searching for a podcast to join me on my drives to practices, I stumbled upon Total Football Analysis. Without any need for convincing, I became a subscriber to the website and a regular listener of the podcasts.

Their ads for tactical writers flashed across my screen for months, but it wasn't until August 2019 that I reached out to Chris Darwin. We got in contact, I wrote my trial analysis and became a full-fledged analyst.

It's been quite the ride.

In that time, I've worked on projects for top-tier clubs in three continents, become a regular on the Total Football Analysis La Liga podcast, led the Real Madrid Prospectus project, and currently offer analyst services to a professional club.

Covering Real Madrid for the majority of the season, I figured, "Why not write a book?"

This book is more than a tactical analysis. It's the product of a year of study, of hundreds of hours analyzing Real Madrid's tactics and player combinations.

Between the reinforcements the club brought in and Zidane's return, there was a lingering thought that this could be a special season.

Though it didn't play out as I initially thought (who would have thought they'd become one of Europe's best defensive teams?), Zidane's tactical innovation, a deeply underappreciated quality, served as more than a return to grace. It was a revitalization.

Breaking down the word, to revitalize is to give new life.

2018/19 Real Madrid was a defeated team. Three coaches and a number of humiliations, especially against their eternal rival, Barcelona, hollowed the team's soul. A shell of their former selves, new life was needed.

It came in the form of new players and, more importantly, the return of Zinedine Zidane, the World Cup winner and club legend.

This book tells the story of the rise, fall, and revitalization of Real Madrid.

Through tactical descriptions and data visualization, I'll walk you through Los Blancos' season, highlighting many of the tactical and statistical themes that returned the La Liga crown to Madrid.

To help me present the story, I recruited Jamie Brackpool to design the cover, capturing a fallen Madrid and the coach to pull them back up to the club's standard.

I've also solicited the help of Sathish Prasad V.T. for his coding, data, and visualization expertise. You'll find more information about him in the back of the book, but, suffice it to say he's a wunderkind in the soccer analysis world. I'm still trying to find a data visualization that will stump him. Check out his profile at the back of the book for more information on his TFA and personal endeavors.

Finally, thank you to my wife for her support, patience, and editing. It pays to marry an English literature major.

Dad, thank you for sharing your time and knowledge with me. I'll never forget your coaching and waking up at 2 a.m. to watch the World Cup and Euros with you. Mom, thank you for shuttling me to and from so many practices and games. I can still hear your cheering from the sideline.

To my in-laws, thank you for your encouragement and support in my entrepreneurial journeys.

Also, thank you to the TFA team, especially Chris Darwin for bringing me into the team and trusting me with some massive projects, David Seymour for his mentorship in those early days, Chris Mumford for his guidance throughout the book writing process, and a host of other analysts for your friendship and community.

Finally, to "The Podcast", I appreciate you guys and enjoy our back-and-forths. Looking forward to taking the pod global.

Now, kick back and enjoy.

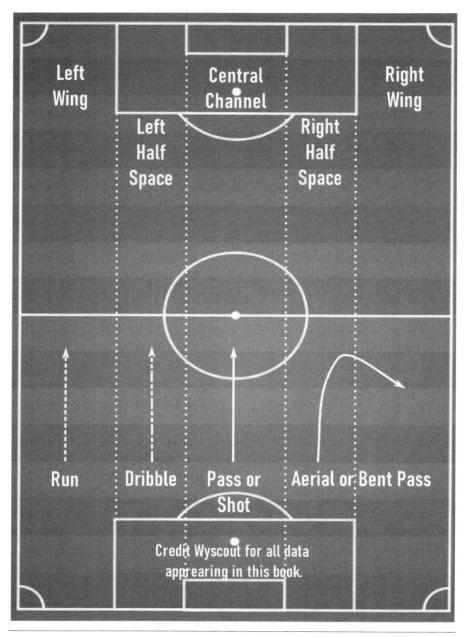

# Chapter 1

# Zidane's First Stint at the Club

Walking down the tunnel after a third consecutive UEFA Champions League trophy, Cristiano Ronaldo's departure was more than a mere walk to the changing room. Rather it was a sign of the times.

Following the game, Ronaldo spoke of his desire to leave Madrid, to find a new adventure, a new challenge in another league. Though captain Sergio Ramos rebuked him for his comment and said that they would settle the matter inside the club, the decision was already made. Cristiano Ronaldo would leave the club.

Before Ronaldo announced his new destination, Zinedine Zidane made the shock announcement that he too was leaving Real Madrid. Rundown after a string of incredible success, the weight of those three Champions League prizes had taken its toll on the Frenchman. Though he and Florentino Pérez were on good terms, with the president even urging him to stay, Zidane took a much-needed rest after an unprecedented level of success.

As Zizou made his parting comments, he cited a need for change at the club: "After three years Real Madrid needs a change, another way of working, another idea, if we are to continue winning. I feel it's going to be difficult to continue winning. And because I'm a winner, I'm going."

Underneath the success, the trophies, and the aura of the Real Madrid way, Zidane and Ronaldo had seen more than those of us on the periphery.

They saw a club increasingly reliant upon aging players.

They saw a side that, after three consecutive years achieving the highest honor in Europe, was showing signs of psychological and physical fatigue.

Zidane had mentioned he was having issues getting anything out of the players. When a coach loses his impact on the players, it's a sign that it's time for him to move on. Well, either he or the players must move on. Moving the players was never going to happen. The side had far too much success together and the players were, in fact, the faces of the team.

That said, new faces were needed, and it seemed unlikely that the club was going to bring in the players from Zidane's transfer list. When his leading goal-scorer, the legendary Ronaldo, walking out the door, it was clear that Zidane would be hamstrung by the absence of his top goal-scoring threat.

But before we get to the 2018/19 season, let's take a look at Zidane's first spell at the club. Examining his first two-and-a-half seasons at the helm gives a clear picture of the standard he set, as well as the club's demise and revitalization.

Rafael Benítez's uninspiring stay at the club, as well as his heavy defeat at the hands of Barcelona, opened the door for Zinedine Zidane to grab the managerial reins. In 2 1/2 years, he managed to win 3 Champions League titles and one La Liga crown.

Under his guidance, Real Madrid put on scintillating attacking displays in both La Liga and the Champions League. In the latter, their success came largely at the expense of Europe's giants.

*Real Madrid's 2017/18 Stats under Zidane*

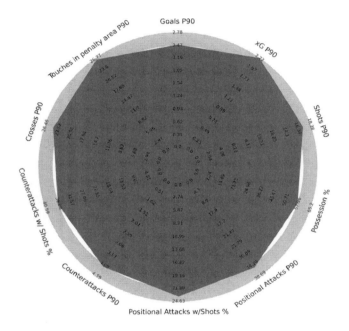

Note that additional radars, both for coaches and players, can be found in the appendix. With the coaching radars, the maximum values were taken from Zidane's two stints with the club, as well as the Lopetegui and Solari team stats.

So when Zidane's 2017/18 attacking stats show the radar reaching the endpoints in touches in the penalty area per 90 minutes and xG per 90, those values represent the best marks in the category over the past five seasons among Real Madrid coaches.

Comparing Zidane's 2017/18 attacking radar with each of the other coaches' attacking stats, it's clear to see that this Real Madrid side was exceptional in the attacking third, especially in their ability to produce quality scoring opportunities. More importantly, it was also a very well-rounded attacking side, garnering high marks across the board.

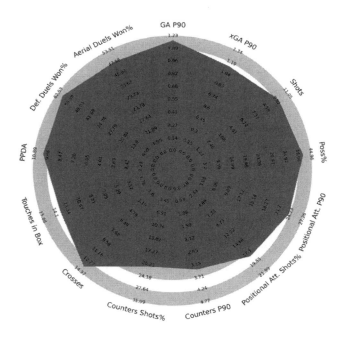

The defensive radar tells another story. While the stats aren't terrible, the side had seen a regression from the previous two seasons. Goals against per 90 continued to rise. During the 2015/16 season, Real Madrid conceded an average of 0.89 goals P90 and 1.17 xGA P90. Those numbers rose to 1.08 GA and 0.95 xGA in 2016/17, then to 1.16 GA and 1.09 xGA the following year.

After controlling the opposition's counterattacks very well during the 2016/17 campaign, allowing 2.79 P90 with 0.58 resulting in shots (21%), Real Madrid allowed 3.61 counterattacks for 90 minutes in 2017/18, with 0.82 shots per game, good for a 23% success rate.

The defensive lapses were coming to the surface; this was an attack first team that went into each match expecting to score two or more goals.

Galáctico expectations are different. Winning wasn't enough.

For Zidane's Real Madrid, the expectation was to win while dominating. Looking at historic Real Madrid sides, as well as the club's identity, no other means were acceptable. That's why, when a coach does arrive, the pressure for success is so intense. As Benítez and Santiago Solari discovered, a strong win percentage isn't enough to keep you on the job. The team had to perform at a certain standard and entertain the fans.

That's exactly where Zidane's Real Madrid excelled.

The most pivotal player on Zidane's side was none other than Cristiano Ronaldo. For nearly a decade, the Portuguese shattered nearly every Real Madrid scoring record. The rivalry between him and Messi, which was itself a microcosm of the Real Madrid versus Barcelona rivalry, set an incredible standard in the Spanish capital.

*Cristiano's Final Years*

In the book, including the side-by-side comparisons in the appendix, the player radar values are specifically tailored to show either a four-year individual performance (as with Kroos and Carvajal) or set values by tactical roles (which is determined for the Real Madrid's forwards, both past and present).

Ronaldo and the current group of forwards set the standards for this radar. If a high value was recorded, that mark became the standard for the data set. All radar stats are strictly from La Liga play. If Champions League contributions were included, Cristiano Ronaldo's goal contributions would move the endpoints of the radar even further.

The above shows us Ronaldo's 2015/16 season in stats. In terms of goal contributions, which includes his La Liga goals and assists for the season, we see that his tally of 46 is the highest marker in the sample.

Other stats that stand out are his goals, shots, and xG per 90 minutes.

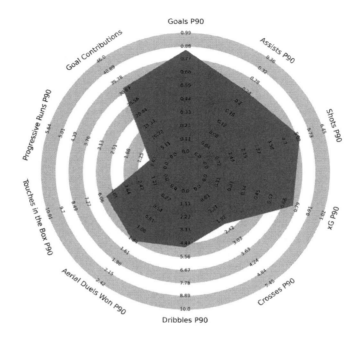

During the 2016/17 campaign, we saw a drop off in his goal score exploits and a slight drop in shots per 90, but it is important to remember that his 2015/16 goal contribution and goals per 90 were unrivaled in the data set.

In fact, in terms of goal contributions, his last two seasons at Real Madrid rated second and third-best among the dataset.

# Cristiano Ronaldo
## 2017/18

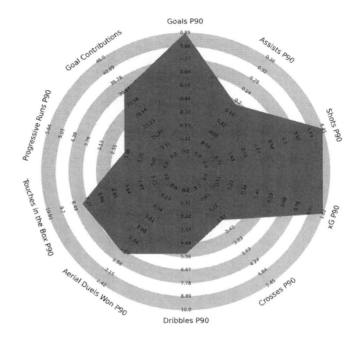

The main differences between his final two seasons at Real Madrid are that his 2017/18 goals, xG, and shots per 90 improved despite lower overall totals. Somehow, 33-year-old Ronaldo was even more active and efficient in the box than he had been the two previous seasons. So, while his goal contributions dropped off, that's largely due to the injuries and rotations he experienced over the course of the year.

Zidane made an effort to keep him fresh in the late stages of the season, resting the Portuguese during La Liga matches to ensure he was fresh for the vital Champions League games. Though there was a dip in his total La Liga output, keeping Ronaldo's legs fresh was a critical piece of Real Madrid's three consecutive Champions League titles, a first in the modern era.

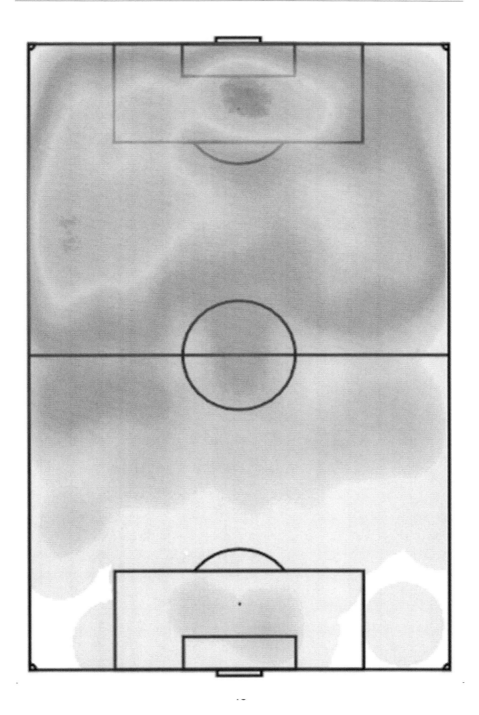

As you studied Ronaldo's season radars, you likely keyed in on the fact that his progressive runs, assists, and crosses per 90 were rather low in comparison to the other Real Madrid forwards.

You'll see the stark contrast in radars as the rest are unveiled (or by skipping forward to the appendix), but, turning our attention to Ronaldo's heat map from the 2017/18 season, we get a glimpse of his utilization in Zidane's system.

As the primary goal scorer on the team, Ronaldo's heat map shines brightest in the very middle of the box, just between the penalty spot and the 6-yard box. While he certainly has a strong presence in the left-wing and half space, and in the right half space to a lesser degree, it's clear the emphasis was to get the club's all-time leading scorer in positions where he could positively impact the game as a goal-scorer.

Given Karim Benzema's frequent movements into the left half space, the Ronaldo-Benzema combination proved lethal for Real Madrid. As primary and secondary goal-scorers for the team, the two worked in tandem to overwhelm opponents, first on the left side of the pitch, then again in the box.

Since the objective was to get Ronaldo into goal-scoring positions, Benzema influenced the game by sliding into the left half space as the team entered the attacking third, then engaging the centerbacks as Real Madrid looked to enter the box. As he initiated contact with the centerbacks, especially if he could pull the opponent's right-centerback close to the left-centerback, pockets of space emerged in the box for Ronaldo to make his runs. If Ronaldo was left against an outside-back, or even a back-peddling centerback, the most an opponent could do was pray the Portuguese would miss the target or receive poor service.

But, with the likes of Gareth Bale, Marcelo, and Dani Carvajal providing service into the box, Ronaldo always had a chance to do some damage. The Portuguese's late runs into the box were incredibly difficult for defenders to track and allowed him to adapt his run to the trajectory of the ball, timing his arrivals to perfection. With defenders already in deep positions, they were unable to slow the momentum of his run and found it difficult to contest his shot.

*Setting Europe's Standard*

With Ronaldo leading the way and the BBC claiming the plaudits from one match to the next, Real Madrid enjoyed its most successful spell in the modern era.

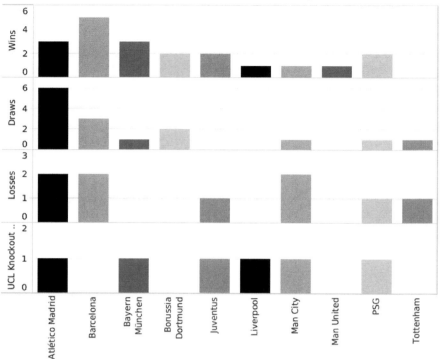

Zidane's Record against Europe's Elites

Under Zidane's guidance, the BBC (Bale-Benzema-Cristiano) led the club to unprecedented success. Zidane's record against Europe's elites speaks for itself.

The benchmark for Real Madrid's success is Champions League and La Liga titles. In order to claim those trophies, odds are you'll need success against Barcelona, Real Madrid's arch-nemesis.

During his first tenure at the club, Zidane locked horns with Barcelona on 10 occasions, claiming five victories and three draws.

Interestingly, it was Atlético Madrid that gave him the most issues. His first spell at the club saw his sides claim three wins, six draws, and two losses. However, most importantly, he did manage to defeat them en route to a Champions League title. While Diego Simeone's men always gave Zidane headaches, they couldn't keep him from winning club soccer's most prestigious competition.

Despite the three consecutive Champions League victories and a La Liga title during his first two and a half seasons as Real Madrid's head coach, Zidane saw the cracks in the system.

With Ronaldo heading to Juventus and an aging squad left without their primary goal scorer, Zidane knew he would have to account for lost goals and patch a leaky defense.

Between the burnout of managing at the highest level for the biggest club in the world, the need to restack the roster, and the complacency brought on by the club's success, Zidane recognized he needed some time away from the game. On May 31st, 2018, Zidane announced he would not return for the following season. Ronaldo followed shortly thereafter, leaving Real Madrid with an identity crisis on their hands.

## Chapter 2

# Lost Identity

*The Tragic Tale of Julen Lopetegui*

As the two club legends walked out the Bernabéu doors, Julen Lopetegui walked in. With his entrance, there was controversy. Pérez signed him from the Spanish national team, a post he held heading into the World Cup. However, Pérez did not initiate proceedings through the Spanish Football Federation, leaving RFEF with no choice but to release him from his contract and move on to a new coach in the days leading up to the World Cup.

The shame and humiliation of his transfer of post from the Spanish national team to Real Madrid hung over Lopetegui like a dark cloud.

It followed him into his new position and increased the pressure for him to succeed. His time at Real Madrid needed to be a resounding success to justify the way his firing from the Spanish national team had occurred. After all, Spain was one of the favorites to lift the World Cup.

Unfortunately for Lopetegui, the cloud remained steadily fixed above his head, following him and his team through his short tenure at the club. Despite scintillating displays in the first few games at the helm, Real Madrid struggled to convert their opportunities. As the gap between Real Madrid and Barcelona widened at the top of the table, pressure mounted on the Spanish coach and his core group of veterans.

*Asking Bale for the Moon*

To some extent, the inability to replace Ronaldo, or at least find someone who could plug the hole, loomed large in Madrid. Rather than investing in a replacement, there was a sense that Ronaldo's departure signaled it was Bale's time to shine, his time to move away from Ronaldo's shadow and into the limelight. Though he was coming off of another injury-plagued season, the club staked their hopes on a healthy, career-best season from the Welshman, expecting him to fill the void left by the Portuguese.

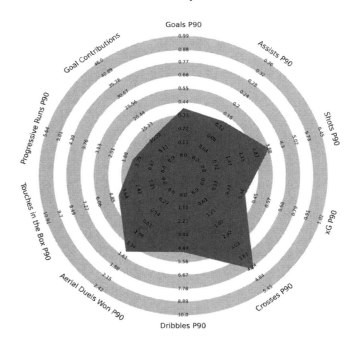

# Gareth Bale
## 2018/19

But that didn't happen.

As Bale picked up five injuries that season, the club scrambled to fill not only Ronaldo's void but Bale's as well. Lucas Vázquez was thrust into the starting right-forward position, Isco received starts on the left side, and the bright young talent, Vinícius Júnior, was given spot starts at left-forward prior to rupturing a ligament in his knee.

Regardless of the combination of players on the pitch, Lopetegui ran into the same issues match after match; the club's leaky defense and inconsistencies in front of goal caused them to drop points, even against teams from the bottom half of the table.

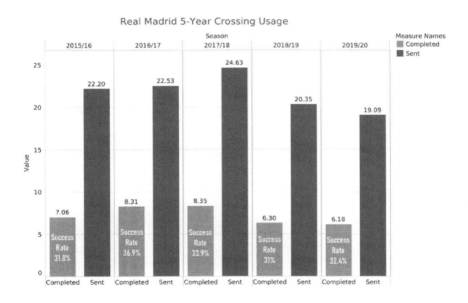

In terms of the attacking vulnerabilities, the loss of Ronaldo and Bale's frequent injuries explains much of the issue. When you look at Lopetegui's teams they are very reliant on crosses. Without Bale and Ronaldo, two of the team's three best aerial threats over the previous few seasons, the side was simply unable to get on the end of crosses. That left Karim Benzema as the lone aerial threat in the box. While he's an excellent target in the box, Big Benz was often double-teamed by the opposing centerbacks. Anything less than perfect service was cleared with ease.

It's not just that Cristiano Ronaldo and Gareth Bale were so proficient in meeting crosses. It was also the chemistry of the BBC in the box that made them so dangerous. That understanding of movements within the box, understanding who goes first, where he's going, how he tailors his run to get to the spot, when he plans to arrive, and why he's making that specific run takes time. Prime BBC had that understanding.

There's no better example of playing off a teammate in the box than you had with Ronaldo and Benzema. The two were simply phenomenal. When you read about Benzema's new role as a primary scorer and hear him speak of what he had to give up to play with Ronaldo, there's a very clear identity in their relationship and how they look to attack opponents.

Benzema had that "first in the box" role. His job was to attract the attention of at least one, if not both, centerbacks and minimize the amount of space they occupied. In doing so, he created pockets of space in the box for Ronaldo to run into. Ronaldo's late movements into the box went largely untracked by the defense because the opponents, tasked with defending crosses, had to first engage Benzema. Since they had to respect his goal-scoring ability, the backline had to drop so that one centerback could defend against Benz while the other offered coverage and helped set the line.

But that connection was lost and it was Lopetegui who was left to suffer.

*Santiago Solari's Nightmare Week*

On October 29, 2018, Julen Lopetegui was fired. The ax fell just a day after a 5-1 thumping at the Camp Nou. Barcelona held a 2-1 lead until the 74th minute, then erupted for three more goals. Luis Suárez finished the match with a hat-trick, sending Los Blancos back to Madrid dejected and humiliated.

Enter Santiago Solari.

A Real Madrid player from 2000-2005, making 131 appearances for the club, Solari worked his way through the club's youth ranks as a coach before leading the B team, Real Madrid Castilla.

A dynamic winger in his playing days, Solari set out to fix a stagnant attack.

Whereas Lopetegui's Real Madrid averaged 65% possession and relied heavily on crosses, Solari's side reduced their totals in both categories. Under his guidance, Real Madrid averaged 57% possession. Positional attacks P90, which are your standard attacks in open play, dropped by nearly eight per game, but counterattacks P90 jumped from 3.31 under Lopetegui to 4.59 with Solari. Counterattacks ending with shots also increased from 37% to 41% under the new regime.

At the time of writing, Solari's 68.75 win percentage ranks 9th in club history. Overall, the side experienced marked improvements over the Lopetegui reign. Averaging 1.95 goals per 90 minutes while conceding an average of just 1.18, the side looked well on their way to a recovery.

However, underneath the surface, warning signs were present and the already stressed foundation continued to deteriorate.

xG (expected goals) and xGA (expected goals against), especially when taken over a broader sample size, offers a nice, albeit simplified, view of a team's expected performances. They take the historic data of shots taken from any given location, then calculate the percentage of shots that ended up at goals. If a shot has an xG of 0.3, then 30% of shots taken from that location have ended up as goals. The reason I say it's simplified is that it gives the output from a broad sample. For a team like Real Madrid, which boasts some of the greatest players on the planet, the team should realistically overperform their xG in any given season, at least by a small margin.

While that goal differential of +0.77 looks great, the fact is that xG to xGA was just 1.65 to 1.34 under Solari. For most teams, that 1.65 xG is fantastic. However, given the 2.22 xG average under Zidane in 2017/18, it was still a far cry from the club's standards. Plus, an xGA of 1.34 is decent for the average team, but not for Real Madrid.

The 0.31 discrepancy in xG to xGA, as well as the high 1.34 xGA per 90, showed all was not right in Madrid.

Then, it happened.

In a seven-day swing, the facade fell. First, on February 27th, Real Madrid entered the home leg of a Copa del Rey Clásico 1-1 vs Barcelona. At the end of the night, the home crowd left the Estadio Santiago Bernabéu having watched a 3-0 dismantling, one that knocked Madrid out of the tournament.

Three days later, the two sides again met in Madrid for the La Liga rendition of El Clásico. Though the game was much closer, Barcelona walked away with another victory, 1-0 on this occasion. The win essentially secured a La Liga title.

To cap off a disastrous week, a Sergio Ramos-less Real Madrid faced Ajax in the Champions League Round of 16, again in front of the Bernabéu faithful. You'll recall Ramos' intentional yellow card at the end of the first leg against Ajax. With the defending champs expecting to brush aside the young upstarts, Ramos took the yellow to ensure he went into the quarterfinal with a clean card slate.

Without the captain on the pitch, disaster struck.

Humiliated in a 4-1 defeat, Real Madrid threw away the Champions League, La Liga, and the Copa del Rey, all in a single week. Find a worse week in club history. I'll wait.

On the back of three humiliations, Solari got the boot, making way for Zinedine Zidane's return.

*To the Drawing Board*

Before we jump to the 2019/20 campaign, we need to know what Zidane was up against. As mentioned, he thought it would be difficult to win anything with the current squad. An aging spine, coupled with young, inexperienced players left him concerned about the fate of the club. Investment was needed, especially with Cristiano Ronaldo's sale to Juventus, but none arrived.

Zidane's prediction would put Nostradamus to shame. All the issues he hinted at became reality. Let's dive into those tactical and personnel issues.

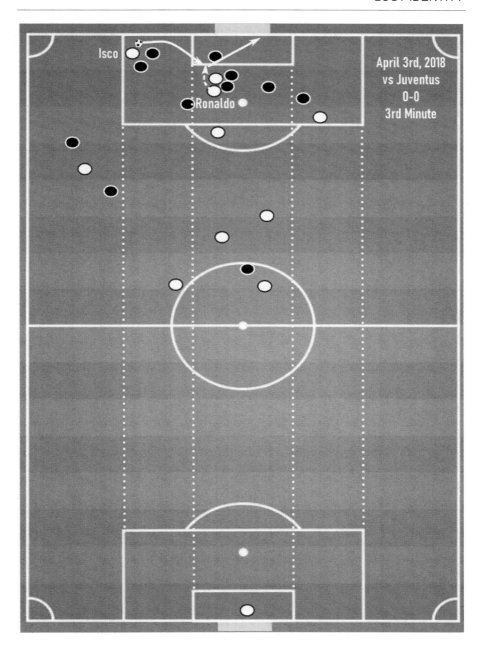

Isco

Ronaldo

April 3rd, 2018
vs Juventus
0-0
3rd Minute

With Benzema increasing the height of the backline, he created additional space for Ronaldo to run into. Frequently lurking near the top of the box, the five-time Ballon d'Or winner waited for the exact moment to initiate the run, the moment where he could arrive at the end of the cross while maximizing his vertical reach. Given that he could outleap the vast majority of opponents, especially with a running start, he targeted the space directly in front of them, cutting off their path to the ball before releasing his shot.

This example comes from Real Madrid's Champions League semifinal tie against Juventus.

Isco had the ball on Real Madrid's left-wing, just inside the box. As he looked for the cross, Benzema was at the near post with Andrea Barzagli and Giorgio Chiellini. Ronaldo was a little bit higher, near the penalty spot.

As Isco sent his cross, both Ronaldo and Benzema started their runs.

On Benzema's part, the run was designed to block off Barzagli and Chiellini's path to the ball. It's definitely a run that's worth watching. The first goal comes in the opening minutes of the game, so you'll see it right away.

In making the run, he allowed Ronaldo to complete his task, a near-post run that cut just in front of Benzema. Had the ball arrived at the Frenchman's foot, Barzagli would likely have blocked the shot. However, with Benzema setting an effective screen, Ronaldo made an unimpeded run to the near post and poked the ball past Gianluigi Buffon for the opening goal of the game.

With the likes of Vázquez, a player who likes to cross the ball, Isco, a playmaker and true 10 who enjoys having the ball at his feet, and Vinícius Júnior, an amazing dribbler with sub-par distributions into the box, the glaring lack of goal-scoring threats was obvious. Benzema was left to do most of the scoring and, while he did produce the majority of Real Madrid's goals, scoring efficiency continued to be an issue.

With playmakers rather than goal-scorers lined up to his left and right, Benzema was forced to adjust his game. Rather than dropping into midfield or even into the wings to switch roles with Ronaldo, Benzema was now the primary scorer. With that change in assignments, his path to goal changed as well.

It was a considerable adjustment for Big Benz, one that he certainly adapted to as the season progressed. But the absence of a secondary scorer plagued the team.

Worse than their attacking issues was their defensive vulnerability. This was one of the problem areas you'd have to assume Zidane recognized before he left the club. Especially in his last season, Marcelo's inability to track back and Ramos' surge into the midfield caused issues for Real Madrid. With Casemiro as the lone holding midfielder and Varane left to cover the void left by Ramos, the back end of Real Madrid's tactics needed a facelift.

This was something Lopetegui did not recognize soon enough. Marcelo continued to start on the left side, relieved of most defensive responsibilities, but the tactics around him were not adapted to compensate for his lack of defensive contribution.

You see, Lopetegui spoke of a romanticized version of football. His side would play an expansive 4-3-3, dominate possession for long spells of time, and continue to produce the prolific goal numbers of recent seasons, even without Ronaldo.

Well, at least that was the intention. The reality was far different.

While Lopetegui's sides did tend to dominate possession and created enough goal-scoring opportunities to get results, it was the side's sloppy defensive tactics that were his undoing.

Let's connect the tactical dots.

Ramos and Varane served as the base of the formation with Casemiro playing just in front of them. Marcelo and Carvajal received the majority of the starts at outside-back, maintaining high and wide starting points throughout the team's attacking phases. Since Real Madrid played point down in the midfield (one defensive midfielder playing under two central attacking mids), Modrić and Kroos typically started high up the pitch to prioritize their connection with the forwards and outside-backs. The forwards would span from half space to half space as the outside-backs progressed up the pitch, leaving the high and wide starting points they held at the start of the possession.

*Where Did Lopetegui and Solari Go Wrong?*

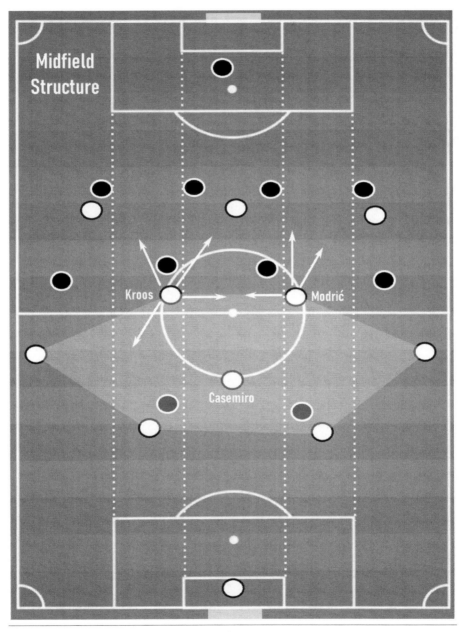

And this is where we really delve into the heart of the matter. With Real Madrid playing a standard 1-4-3-3 with two attacking midfielders and outside-backs who pushed high and wide to support the outside forwards, Madrid was effectively asking Casemiro to cover the full width of the pitch in his attempts to protect the backline.

When you look at the midfielders' movement, Kroos would occasionally drop deep into the left half space, but he and Modrić typically either moved high up the pitch or more centrally depending on the positioning of the ball.

As the lone midfielder behind the ball, Casemiro was often asked to cover the full width of the pitch and was the only player situated between the attacking midfielders and centerbacks. Given the expansive attacking tactics of both Lopetegui and Solari, opponents found success playing into the half spaces behind Modrić and Kroos, which allowed them to run at Casemiro. With the Brazilian forced to step into the midfield to contest the opponent's attack, the opposition could target the momentum of his forward movement to play the ball around him. Even if Casemiro was well set and ready to run into the space behind him, opponents running into that space at full speed always had the advantage.

That in turn impacted the actions of Ramos and Varane. One option, which hurt them quite often during the 2018/19 campaign, was to step into midfield to contest the initial pass behind Casemiro. The second was to backtrack and attempt to delay the attack, more cautious but also buying additional time to respond.

Watching every scoring opportunity Real Madrid conceded that season, it was interesting to see how frequently Ramos decided to contest the opponent's progression in the middle third.

When it worked, the side was able to reclaim possession and restart attacks. When it didn't, the results were devastating. That expansive rest defense, the team shape when they had possession of the ball, left them vulnerable in transitional moments. As Ramos stepped into midfield, counterattacking gaps emerged across the back.

That's where Lopetegui's Real Madrid met their demise. The team's inability to quickly counterpress, deny progressive passes, and recover numbers behind the ball meant the opposition only needed two or three opportunities a game to secure their goals. The goal-scoring chances Real Madrid conceded were very high quality, due in large part to the vast amount of space they covered when in possession. Without the midfield and outside-backs well-positioned to recover defensively and get behind the ball, opponents patiently awaited Real Madrid's mistakes, then pounced en route to goal.

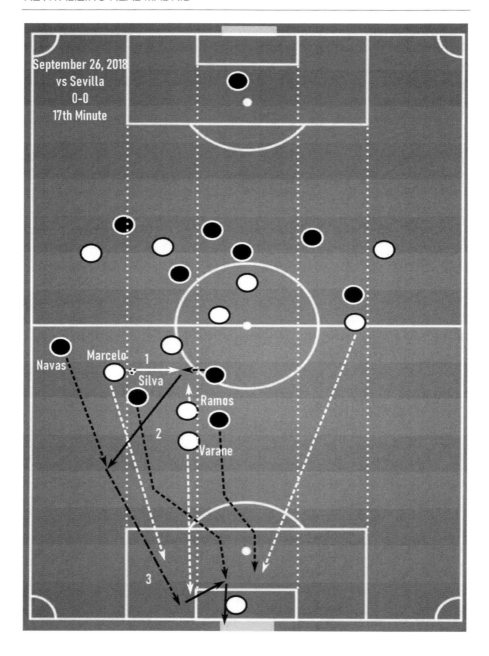

September 26, 2018
vs Sevilla
0-0
17th Minute

Navas
Marcelo 1
Silva
Ramos
2
Varane
3

Here, we have an example from Real Madrid's early-season match against Sevilla. Marcelo played a poor pass into the left half space, which was intercepted by Sevilla. Once the turnover was made, Marcelo stood in place and ball-watched while Jesús Navas began his run down the wing.

With Sevilla engaged in a 4v4 against Real Madrid in that area of the field, they were first to the ball, beating out the oncoming run of Ramos. With Ramos moving into midfield to contest the loose ball and Marcelo sitting back where he played the initial pass, a large gap emerged between Marcelo and Ramos, allowing Sevilla to play the ball into Navas in the wing.

The former Manchester City winger made his run behind the Real Madrid line, sprinting deep into the half space before Varane could cut off his path to goal. However, with Varane now shifted into the left half space to contest the run of Navas, Sevilla now had two players wide open in the middle of the box.

It was André Silva's near-post run that Navas picked out, completing a negative (read as passing backward) pass to the Portuguese for an easy finish. Not only was Marcelo responsible for the turnover, but he also failed to track the run of Navas, allowing the Spaniard to run freely into the wings.

Ramos' role cannot be ignored either. Stepping aggressively into midfield, he effectively engaged in an all or nothing, high-risk encounter despite not having a chance at the tackle. Had he dropped off and looked to delay the attack, he would have bought time for Marcelo and the midfield to recover.

While aggression is a key component of centerback play, the quality of a player's risk analysis can save a goal or gift one. In this instance, Ramos was in a giving mood.

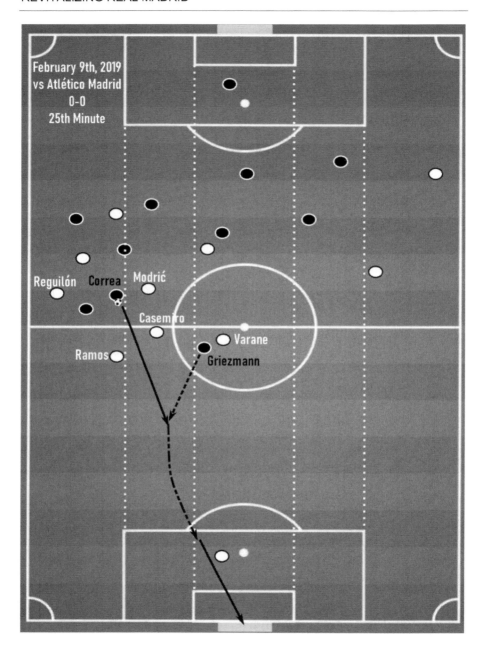

February 9th, 2019
vs Atlético Madrid
0-0
25th Minute

Reguilón   Correa   Modrić

Casemiro

Varane

Ramos   Griezmann

While Marcelo certainly deserves some of the blame for the side's defensive woes, especially since tracking back into the team's defensive structure has never been a strength of his, this type of situation isn't specific to Marcelo. The youngster, Sergio Reguilón, was caught in a very similar predicament against Atlético Madrid.

Atlético set a midfield line of confrontation, getting 11 players behind the ball. Antoine Griezmann was the lone forward up top. As he pressed Ramos and Varane, he had six teammates behind him denying entry to five Real Madrid players in that same zone.

When Atlético recovered the ball, Reguilón was caught in a high and wide position, leaving him unable to counterpress. Ángel Correa was able to quickly pick out the run of Griezmann. The Frenchman's run split Ramos and Varane. Since Ramos was playing a little deeper than his partner, Griezmann started a few yards ahead of Varane and had the benefit of starting his run before his compatriot.

The result is pretty straightforward. Griezmann took his first touch as he entered the final third, entered the box uncontested, and nutmegged Courtois for the opening goal of the game.

Though Los Blancos would ultimately come back and win this match 3-1, this sequence is a sign of a bigger tactical issue that was present during Zidane's last season, one that went unanswered under the new coaching staff. Failure to address the half space distribution points proved to be an Achilles' heel. Without the scoring exploits of Cristiano Ronaldo to save the team, the side was simply unable to continue scoring at an otherworldly rate to account for their defensive fragilities.

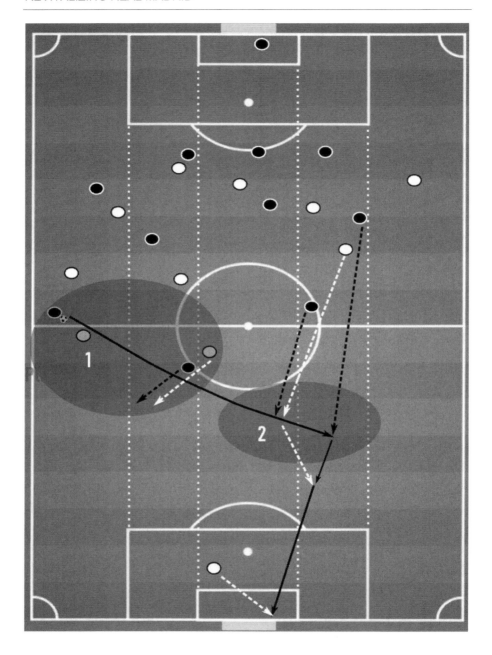

Issues on the left side of the pitch were frequent. A broken record couldn't repeat a sequence better than Real Madrid's continuous exposure against the counterattack.

With Marcelo engaged in the attack higher up the pitch, massive amounts of space emerged just in front of Sergio Ramos. Opponents looked to play into the space just in front of Ramos, pulling him into the midfield. In the image, there are two shaded areas. The first, which has a number one on it, shows where opponents targeted Real Madrid. As Ramos moved wide to cover for Marcelo, Varane was forced to slide to his left in coverage of Ramos. That vicious circle of defensive coverage left the right side exposed if Carvajal was engaged higher up the pitch. With Bale operating as the team's attacking focal point high on the right, Carvajal often moved higher up the pitch to give Real Madrid the high and wide overload.

If the counterpress was unsuccessful and Marcelo was still positioned high up the pitch, which he typically was in Lopetegui and Solari's expansive attacking tactics, that meant opponents could quickly switch play into Real Madrid's left half space, targeting the space between Marcelo and Ramos.

Poor rest defense forced Real Madrid to scramble after a loss of possession. With that triangle of Casemiro, Ramos, and Varane forced to cover the full width of the pitch, opponents found success targeting the half spaces just in front of Ramos and Varane, especially on the left-hand side.

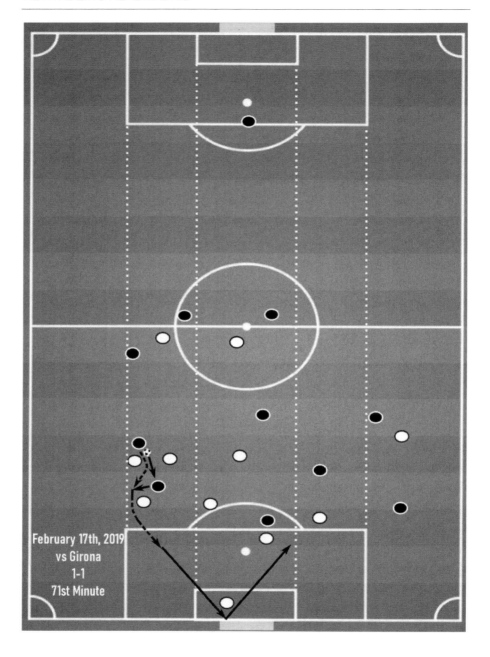

February 17th, 2019
vs Girona
1-1
71st Minute

Even during the opposition's open possessions, a lack of defensive awareness and failure to track runners continued to hurt Real Madrid.

In the sequence above, Girona had possession of the ball in Real Madrid's defensive third. On the surface, the situation looks fairly benign. In the immediate vicinity of the ball, Los Blancos enjoyed a 3v2 advantage. Centrally, the side had a 3v1 numerical edge.

However, a simple give-and-go allowed Girona to win the 2v3 situation, getting behind both Marcelo and Ramos.

Since Madrid was defending on the edge of the box, winning that 2v3 immediately put Girona in shooting position. The shot clanged off the crossbar, preserving the 1-1 scoreline.

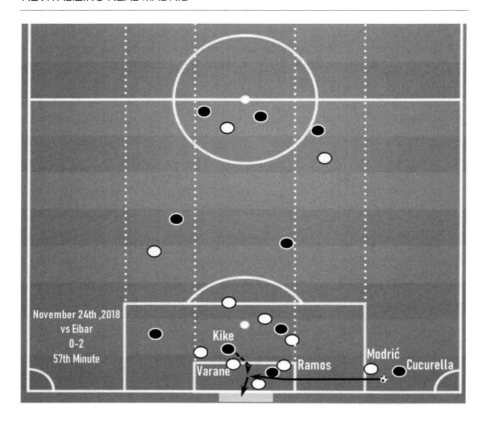

While the side's lack of discipline and structure was most evident in the middle third of the pitch, backline movement in the defensive third was an issue as well.

In their match against Eibar, Barcelona loanee Marc Cucurella had the ball on Real Madrid's right-wing, not far from the corner kick spot.

Modrić closed him down, leaving Cucurella with either a negative pass or a hopeful cross into the box.

At the very least, it gave the appearance of the hopeful ball since Real Madrid had plenty of numbers in the box to defend against the cross.

Taking a deeper look, Ramos and Varane had switched sides with each other, leaving Ramos at the near post. As the delivery arrived at the near post, Ramos was behind his mark, who was onside. Suspecting a shot at the near post, Courtois moved to his right to contest the shot. However, the cross was dummied, allowing it to reach the middle of the box.

Varane's positioning was perfect, but he was caught off guard by the dummy. Unfortunately for Real Madrid, Kike wasn't.

He made a nice run around Varane, beating the Frenchman to the cross and producing a third goal for the underdogs.

Giving credit where it's due, the decision to dummy and the run around Varane were nice pieces of attacking play from Eibar. That said, Ramos' poor positioning and Varane's lack of awareness of Kike's run were equally responsible for the goal. In this situation, where a team has numbers prepared to defend the cross, there is simply no excuse for getting beaten by a simple delivery and losing track of runners in the heart of the box.

Though this is just one goal, It is symptomatic of the lack of defensive structure, discipline, and awareness that ran rampant at Madrid. Neither Lopetegui nor Solari managed to solve the side's defensive woes, leading to their dismissal and the return of Zidane.

## Chapter 3

# The Return of Zidane - A Revitalization

Following another Clásico loss to Barcelona and a Champions League exit in the Round of 16 to a young, upstart Ajax team, Santiago Solari was given the boot.

His replacement...none other than Zinedine Zidane.

With the club in dire need of course correction and Zidane on great terms with Florentino Pérez, Real Madrid brought its most successful manager back into the fold.

Upon reclaiming the helm on March 11th, 2019, Zidane would spend the remaining three months of the season analyzing the club's needs and working towards his tactical solutions for the following season. Out of the Champions League and Copa del Rey, and virtually out of La Liga, this was the time for experimentation.

*New Signings*

Among the influences in his departure was the club's need for change. Between age and complacency, fresh blood was needed to revitalize this group. He had foreseen 2018/19's issues, but the club did not heed his warning. Rather, they entered the season without significant roster moves and a no-holds-barred attacking philosophy.

One of the conditions Zidane put forward to Pérez was that the club reinvest in the squad, bringing in a mixture of young talent and an established superstar to replace the production of Ronaldo.

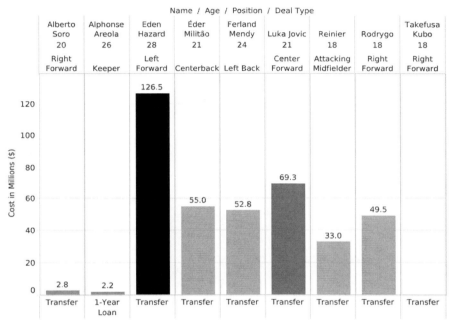

## New Signings

Name / Age / Position / Deal Type

| | Alberto Soro 20 Right Forward Transfer | Alphonse Areola 26 Keeper 1-Year Loan | Eden Hazard 28 Left Forward Transfer | Éder Militão 21 Centerback Transfer | Ferland Mendy 24 Left Back Transfer | Luka Jovic 21 Center Forward Transfer | Reinier 18 Attacking Midfielder Transfer | Rodrygo 18 Right Forward Transfer | Takefusa Kubo 18 Right Forward Transfer |
|---|---|---|---|---|---|---|---|---|---|

Cost in Millions ($): 2.8, 2.2, 126.5, 55.0, 52.8, 69.3, 33.0, 49.5

Those young stars took the form of the impressive young Serbian, Luka Jović, Porto's Éder Militão, a pair of Brazilian attackers in Rodrygo and Reinier, Alberto Soto, and the former Barcelona academy product, Takefusa Kubo.

The club spent $209.6 million on those six, an average of $34.9 million per player.

In terms of the more established signings, Eden Hazard was the much-promised superstar. At $126.5 million, he was tabbed to reclaim some of the production lost by Cristiano Ronaldo's departure. With Hazard on the left, Benzema in the middle, and Bale on the right, Real Madrid were confident the goals would return.

In terms of repairing the side's broken defensive system, the club brought in Ferland Mendy from Lyon. A hard-working left-back with an extraordinary attention to detail in the defensive phases of the game, the young Frenchman had also put on a blistering attacking performance against Barcelona in the Champions League.

The last major signing was also of the defensive mold, bringing in Alphonse Areola to replace Keylor Navas as the backup goalkeeper. You could argue that this move was really about fully transferring the starting goalkeeping responsibilities from Navas to Courtois.

*Repairing a Broken Mindset*

Walking into the locker room as Real Madrid manager for the second time, Zidane needed to fix more than the team's tactics. More importantly, he needed to repair the mindset.

Psychologically, the team looked defeated.

Scoring against Madrid in previous seasons was akin to poking the bear. Sure, you got a shot in, but now you had to fight for your life.

During the 2018/19 season, conceded goals produced poor body posture and a visibly shaken side. It seemed as though opponents knew that if they could find the initial break-through, more goals would follow.

A change in mindset was necessary to pull this group out of its funk. Rather than letting negativity linger, impacting the next series of events, the team did a better job of acknowledging any faults, then refocusing on the present.

Throughout the season, Zidane spoke on the theme of suffering. That's a packed idea.

First, he related suffering to match preparation, which is itself multi-faceted. With a loaded schedule, elite teams use their week for recovery sessions and tactical preparation. Practices are generally low-intensity events as legs are preserved for matches. Training session as a means of conditioning physical suffering is rather straightforward. But how does a manager address this complex topic without hitting the pitch?

For one, building the conversation around the team concept proves fruitful. For a side like Real Madrid, dominant victories are the expectation. However, no one reaches a 10/10 every day. That goes for the team as well. Further, when you're an elite team, opponents circle the fixture date on the calendar. For many clubs, a game against the league's elites is the closest they'll get to the limelight.

With those things in mind, match preparation must address match and opposition expectations. For Real Madrid, it doesn't matter if they're playing Barcelona or Eibar. They have to assume the best version of the opponent will show up on game day. Accepting that you're going to face the opposition's 10/10 opens the floor for dialog. How will they make us suffer? Are there certain strengths they possess that will negatively impact our approach? Will they drop deep and look to make this a miserable, frustrating match?

In a sense, the conversation is intended to activate the negative emotions prior to lacing up the boots and taking the field. Identifying potential issues or stressors then allows the team to start working out the solutions. That process of investigation imparts confidence and encourages a proactive mental state once the match starts. Understanding potential issues and engaging them before the match also serves to calm the nerves.

A coach's demeanor travels. If the coach panics or suffers from uncontrollable anger, the players feel it. The psychological state of the coach then negatively impacts performance, both his and the players.

You won't find many managers with Zidane levels of zen. We've seen the random outburst of emotion from missed sitters, but, on the whole, he conveys total self-control, exudes confidence, and manifests a presence of mind that carries on to the players.

In the mind of a winner, suffering is by necessity. It's the response that matters most. This Real Madrid side seemed more comfortable with suffering. Their demeanor on the pitch is the proof.

The second form of suffering follows from the first. Whereas the first factors into match preparation, the second is teaching the players to manage their mental state in the flow of the game, including the response to individual and collective failures.

Whether the 2019/20 team's improved performances were a matter of greater confidence through better preparation, improved self-talk, Zidane's aura, or some combination of the three, the in-game psychological responses seemed greatly improved. It's fair to say this is simply speculation, but the way a person carries himself offers clues into their character.

The spiraling of the previous season wasn't apparent on the 2019/20 film. Even as the side raced Barcelona through the stretch run, there was always this sense of ownership of their trajectory. It's not that they could control each result, but there was a sense of confidence the club conveyed that is directly tied to their mental models. An event in a game could go against them, so could the result, but the process was never in question.

*2019/20 in Numbers*

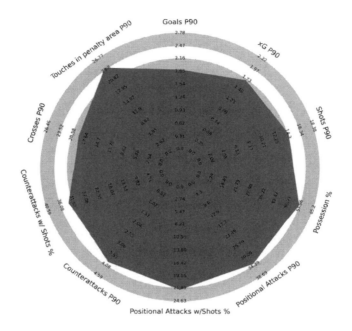

# Zinedine Zidane
## Attacking stats 2019/20

That process directly corresponds to the team's playing philosophy, their identity. With Zidane at the helm, the club's identity was never in question. That's because Zidane knew himself and the club. With that clear image in his mind, he could then show the players how they fit into that picture, a quality of all top coaches and managers, both inside and outside of sports.

Looking at Real Madrid's attacking stats for the 2019/20 season, Zidane's side is not nearly as prolific as his early teams. In fact, any of the categories rate well below previous sides. While they still performed well in the touches in the penalty area per 90 and counterattacks per 90 categories, the star power in the final third was still lacking.

Gareth Bale's injury issues and loss of form certainly hurt the attack on the right-hand side of the pitch, but the more pressing concern was Eden Hazard's frequent injuries. After arriving in Madrid overweight and out of shape during his first preseason, the Belgian struggled mightily to regain his form.

When Hazard was in the squad, his presence did bring an attacking boost, relieving some of the pressure from Benzema's broad shoulders.

However, he would only manage 16 La Liga appearances during his first season with the club, 14 of which were starts. Hazard's absence shifted responsibility to Isco and Vinícius Júnior.

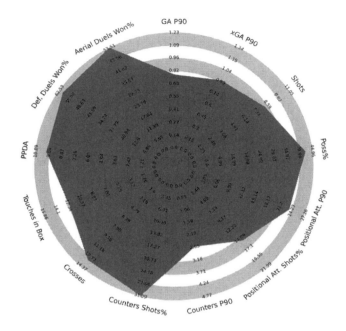

Unlike the Galácticos of old, this Real Madrid side found their success through their prioritization of the defensive phases rather than the attacking set up of the game. Not only was this Zidane's best defensive work at Real Madrid, but his group also ranked among the best in Europe in several defensive categories.

During the 2019/20 season, Real Madrid conceded just 0.66 goals per 90 and an xGA of 0.8. Opponents averaged just 8 shots per game, 2.79 found the target. Key to their defensive success was the way they controlled their opponent's counterattacking capabilities. On a per match basis, opponents averaged 2.55 counterattacks with just 0.79 culminating in a shot. The 31% success rate is high, but given the low number of counterattacks, the lack of volume more than compensates for the high percentage.

Without Cristiano Ronaldo, an in-form Bale, and a healthy Hazard, Zidane was forced to lean on his defensive tactics. Without the guarantee of two plus goals per game, the side would have to find a new way to win.

This is where the revitalization begins.

Without the comforts of multiple prolific goal scorers, Zidane had to introduce a layer of pragmatism into the club's style of play. Rather than the all-out attacking of the Lopetegui and Solari sides, Zidane's tactics started with defensive security. He saw the issues in the half spaces, particularly on the left, so he added a layer of protection in front of the backline. Opponents would no longer enjoy free runs at Sergio Ramos and Raphaël Varane.

Fixing Real Madrid's rest defense was the first item on the agenda.

*Chapter 4*

# Zidane's Biggest Fix - Rest Defense

If there's a single common theme in the previous two chapters, it's that the 2018/19 side really struggled defensively and that Zidane recognized that Real Madrid's defensive tactics were the single greatest obstacle standing between the club and trophies. Containing the opposition's counterattacking was the primary concern. With the decrease in goals, the club had to improve on the other side of the ball.

Browse the internet for five minutes and you'll find a number of different opinions for Real Madrid's sudden defensive improvements.

Some will point to the impact Ferland Mendy has had on the left-wing. Others will say that Sergio Ramos had a career year. You also find references to Federico Valverde's energy in midfield and Vinícius Júnior's work higher up the pitch.

Though the individual player contributions certainly made an impact, the most influential reason for Real Madrid's defensive success was Zinedine Zidane's adjustments to the team's rest defense.

As mentioned earlier, a team's rest defense is their positional organization when they have possession of the ball. So if Benzema has possession of the ball in the opponent's half of the field just inside of the left half space, the positioning of the players around him is what makes up the team's rest defense.

A good rest defense is what allows teams to quickly transition from an open possession to counterpressing. Teams with a strong sense of positional play structure themselves to allow for greater ease of transition. On the whole, the philosophy of positional play produces greater structure on both the attacking and defensive sides of the ball, while strengthening a team's transitional play.

So, what were the big changes?

First, moving away from the point down midfield system, Zidane restructured his midfield, moving Kroos into a regista role, much like we saw with Andrea Pirlo throughout his marvelous career.

Since opponents had made a habit of targeting Real Madrid's left half space, Zidane looked for a way to continue utilizing his left-back in a more advanced role while giving him coverage against the counterattack. That solution was to move Kroos into a deeper role. As opponents settled into their middle and low blocks, you would often find Kroos just beyond the opposition's press. By positioning himself outside their defensive structure, Kroos had the two-fold benefit of having additional time and space to complete his attacking actions, as well as a deeper starting point to deny opponents free access to Real Madrid's left half space.

*The Central Square*

With Kroos in a deeper starting position, Real Madrid had a deep central square with Casemiro, Sergio Ramos, and Raphaël Varane rounding out the other points. Instead of asking Casemiro to cover the whole width of the pitch, this central square put Kroos in a position where he could cover the left half space and wing, reducing Casemiro's coverage area to three of the five vertical channels, the central channel, right half space, and right-wing.

This new square made Ramos' life easier as well. Unlike the previous season, where he was essentially asked to cover the entire left half of the field with little to no help, Kroos' placement reduced the need for Ramos to move into midfield. Now, he still made those aggressive forward moves to pressure the ball, but Kroos' presence reduced the number of times these moves occurred and greatly improved Ramos' efficiency when he made those midfield runs.

With Ramos now free to maintain a stay-at-home role, the space Varane was asked to cover was reduced as well. In the best-case scenario, if Ramos is pulled high into midfield, he's doing so against a lone center forward. Should Ramos either lose the tackle or aerial duel and see the ball played behind him, a more central starting point improves the speed at which Varane can move into a first defender role.

Thanks to the central square, Real Madrid had two players contest the opposition's outlet passes and an additional two players to guard against passes played over the top. Much like Lopetegui and Solari, Zidane still committed numbers high up the pitch, but it was the way he situated his players within the team's rest defense that helped them become one of Europe's best defensive sides.

*To the Drawing Board*

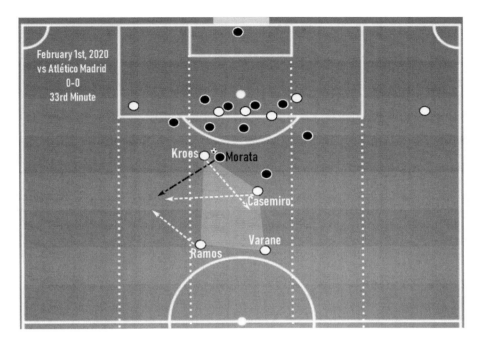

In the home leg against Atlético Madrid, Los Blancos entered the match knowing they had to control their crosstown rival's counterattacking. Diego Simeone's men are well known for their fast-paced, direct attacks, so controlling the early stages of the counterattack was crucial to Real Madrid's success.

In the 33rd minute, the brake was on. Before winning the ball, the side was sitting deep in their end in a low block. In terms of their horizontal reach, Atlético was incredibly compact, spanning from the inner regions of one half space to the other. After recovering the ball deep in their end of the pitch, Atlético initiated the counterattack.

As they looked to break through the first Real Madrid lines, Casemiro was quick to respond, pursuing the ball into Atlético's right half space. A heavy touch from Álvaro Morata pushed the ball further into the wing. At that point, Sergio Ramos took over and was able to end the threat.

The key to Real Madrid's successful counterattack defense was this structure of the rest defense. Remember that a team's rest defense is the positioning of the players when their team still has possession of the ball. For Real Madrid, a side that likes to push six players higher up the pitch as the team looks to make their move to goal, the placement of those other four players give them the difference between a successful counterpress and a conceded goal.

At the very bottom of Real Madrid's formation, you can see a square. At the base are Ramos and Varane, the two centerbacks. Just ahead of them are Casemiro and Kroos. In terms of their orientation, the four players typically cover two out of the five vertical channels. In this particular case, all five were situated in the central channel. This is likely due to Atlético's horizontal compaction. With all of Atlético's field players situated within a 25-yard range, narrow starting positions allowed that Real Madrid square to contest any loose balls that squirted out of the attacking third and also allowed them to eliminate Atlético Madrid's most direct route to goal.

The players' starting positions were perfect. By forcing Morata out into the wings, they put him in a position where he had to engage in a 1v1 duel with Ramos before playing into a teammate. Further, Kroos was positioned roughly in line with Casemiro, when the German was beat and the Brazilian stepped into the first defender (pressure) role, Kroos quickly transitioned and entered Casemiro's zone. That combination of the midfielders allowed Ramos and Varane to maintain their deeper starting points. In turn, Ramos' involvement was more calculated than we've seen in previous examples. By allowing Casemiro to apply the first layer of pressure, Ramos was able to wait for Morata's first touch into the wings. As the forward was forced wide,

Ramos assumed the first defender role. Now that Morata had limited options, Ramos could engage more forcefully and with better timing in the tackle.

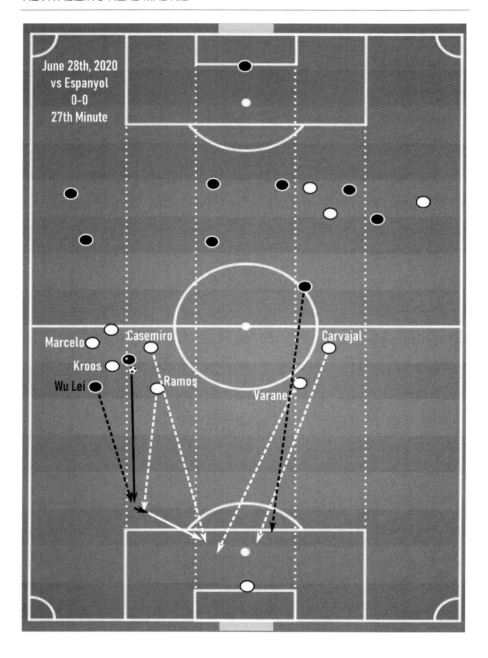

Later in the season, we again saw Ramos coming to the rescue. In the away match against Espanyol, Wu Lei managed to find a pocket of space behind both Kroos and Marcelo. Playing behind the line in his team's right half space, Lei had just one player standing between him in the goal, Sergio Ramos.

In a very similar situation that was outlined in chapter 2, we saw Marcelo commit a turnover and Ramos move aggressively into midfield to apply pressure on the ball carrier. A pass was sent to Jesús Navas who broke behind the Real Madrid line and assisted André Silva's goal.

This scenario is almost identical to the one against Sevilla. However, in this instance, Ramos maintained a deeper starting point, allowing Espanyol to play the run of Lei. Anticipating the pass, Ramos maintained this side-on body orientation (his back facing one of the two sidelines). That orientation placed him in a position where he could either run forward into the midfield or quickly transition into a sprint towards his own goal.

In this instance, he was called to the latter. Since he had the inside track, Ramos prevented Lei from taking an aggressive first touch towards goal. Once the Chinese was forced to slow his progress, his only path to goal was to try cutting inside of Ramos. The Spaniard was prepared to continue his run towards the end line if Lei took a heavy touch, but he was also well prepared for the inside cut. As Lei chopped the ball towards the center of the pitch, Ramos made an excellent tackle to end the Espanyol counterattack.

One other positive to note is the recovery of the other Real Madrid players. Both Casemiro and Varane have quickly tracked back into cover positions with the former even claiming the loose ball. There were also nice recovery runs from Marcelo, Kroos, and Carvajal. At the time of Casemiro's recovery, Real Madrid enjoyed a 6v2 numeric superiority in their defensive third.

Ramos' decision making and tackling technique were spot on, but so were the recoveries of the other Real Madrid players. That's in large part due to Zidane's work on the team's rest defense in counterpressing. In previous years, there was no guarantee the players would have had such strong starting points or put in the work to recover defensively.

But this was a new team.

Without the assurance of multiple goals per game, the team came to take greater pride in their defensive production. With Zidane's tactics securing better starting points for his players, there were simply no excuses for the players. In the event of a defensive breakdown, individuals were now held responsible for their actions in those dangerous transitional moments.

*Front Six in Rest Defense*

With the central square intact, let's move on to the highest players on the pitch. Take away the four players from the central square and Zidane's left with six field players. Of those six field players, two are outside-backs, one is a right-sided central midfielder, and the other three are forwards.

Zidane's attacking tactics will shed more light on his rest defense, but, for the time being, suffice it to say that he looked to connect those six field players through wing and half space overloads.

What do I mean by overload?

As managers prepare for their opponents, the attacking tactics aim to produce superiorities, be it quantitative, qualitative, positional, or socio-affective (think chemistry). Various superiorities can be combined, such as a quantitative and qualitative superiority on the wings.

When Zidane's Real Madrid has an open possession, you will frequently see them overload in the wings and adjacent half spaces. That means he's trying to create a scenario in which his team has more players in one specific area than the other team does.

Even if the opponent manages to get equal numbers into that same area, Zidane's side typically enjoys a qualitative advantage, so a 2v2 scenario is more likely to play out in his team's favor than the opponents. Better players equal a better chance of success.

With that attacking approach in mind, Zidane had to find a way to improve the efficiency of the transition to defense. The previous season, players in high and wide positions were supposed to make that transition from an open attack to the counterpress. In recovering the ball, opponents wanted to break the first line right away. If they were able to do so, they were able to attack open space and run at that triangle of Casemiro, Ramos, and Varane. Improving the team's counterpressing was a priority as was improving their rest defense within their positional play.

While he still had the wing and half space overloads, often placing two or three players in connection with each other, he layered their starting points and improved the way in which they engaged in the counterpress. Plus, with Kroos and Casemiro playing beneath the high and wide overloads, there was greater security in the case of a lost possession.

Between the double pivot of Kroos and Casemiro, as well as the high and wide overloads, Real Madrid had much more success protecting the half spaces. Opponents were unable to play into those spaces as effectively as they had the previous year, which greatly reduced the areas they could attack with their outlet passes. Even if they managed to play into the half space, Real Madrid was well-positioned to answer the new threat.

*To the Drawing Board*

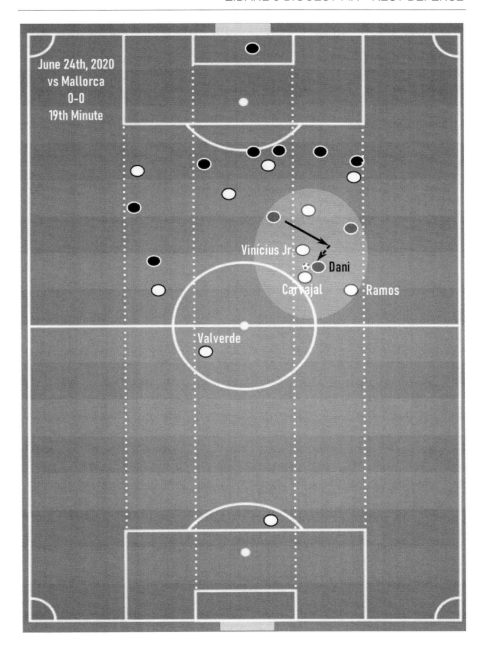

June 24th, 2020
vs Mallorca
0-0
19th Minute

Vinícius Jr.

Dani

Carvajal   Ramos

Valverde

The defensive responsibilities didn't fall exclusively on that central square. Since the team averaged 58% possession per game, much of it coming in the attacking half of the pitch, the whole team had to commit to the counterpress.

A conversation about Zidane's attacking tactics is on the horizon, but, for the sake of this example, suffice it to say they showed a preference for wide overloads, though certainly not to the extent of Lopetegui and Solari. As Madrid searched for gaps in the opposition's low block, it was common to find three Madrid players closely connected on either side of the pitch. As part of the team's rest defense, as well as their general approach to positional play, one player would often occupy the wing, positioning himself very closely to the touchline, another was positioned in half space, and the third looked for pockets of space to play off of the other two. The three players generally maintained a triangular pattern, guaranteeing the possibility of combination play through diagonal passing.

Since we're more concerned with the defensive phases at the moment, the benefit here is that Real Madrid always had a half space presence to engage in the counterpress. If the low block was able to repel Real Madrid's advances to goal, Los Merengues had players well-positioned to quickly counterpress.

In the June 24th match against Mallorca, Real Madrid had just finished taking a corner kick and restarted preparations for box entry when a poor pass led to a turnover.

Since Madrid took the corner short and exchanged a number of passes in the wings prior to the loss, several of the players had already started to retreat into their standard rest defense. The one exception was Federico Valverde, who maintained his place as the deepest player back during corner kicks.

One of the players who had fully regained his rest defense positioning was Dani Carvajal. Since he's not someone who enters the box during corner kicks, his recovery was a fairly easy one. Starting in the right half space, he was quick to read the turnover and respond to Mallorca's forward pass. Just as Mallorca's Dani was about to break free of the press and start his run at Valverde, Carvajal stepped in with a brilliant tackle, ending the counterattack and allowing Valverde to restart possession.

By prioritizing the half space, Carvajal was quick to identify the threat and respond appropriately. Defending in the half spaces, especially against the counterattack, was a major factor in Real Madrid's 2019/20 success. Since Real Madrid went into each match expecting nearly 60% possession, they had to find ways to fend off the opposition's counterattacking opportunities. The central square, as well as the half space occupation of players higher up the pitch, allowed them to control the space available to the opponent in transitional moments. With the opponents under duress and lacking outlets, Real Madrid became one of Europe's stoutest defensive teams.

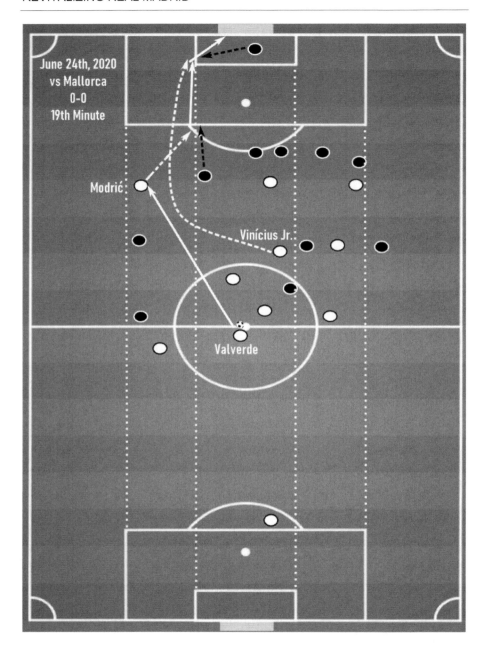

June 24th, 2020
vs Mallorca
0-0
19th Minute

Modrić

Vinícius Jr.

Valverde

Following from that Carvajal tackle, we saw another benefit of a good counterpress, the quick and fluid transition back to the attack.

Real Madrid was incredibly difficult to break down in open possessions. With opponents experiencing so little success in open possessions, they tended to prioritize the counterattack. However, in prioritizing the counterattack, we often saw opponents over commit in those transitional moments. As players rushed upfield to join the attack, attempting to counter before Real Madrid could set their press, a new threat emerged.

Since Real Madrid players were well-situated within their rest defense, they were able to counterpress the opponents rather quickly. As they pressed the opposition, a quick recovery typically gave them a counterattacking situation of their own. Unlike the opponents, who still had 80 yards between the point of recovery and Thibaut Courtois' goal, Real Madrid's high and middle recoveries fell within a range of 30 to 50 yards from goal.

If the opponents began their sprint up the field, Real Madrid was then able to target spaces vacated by the onrushing attackers.

In this sequence from the Mallorca game, Carvajal's pass to Valverde was immediately played forward to Luka Modrić. With the near-sighted opponent streaking forward to join the counterattack, Modrić was left alone on the left side of Real Madrid's formation. He made his move towards goal while also buying time for his teammates to join him in the attack.

From out of nowhere, Vinícius Júnior arrived on the scene, overlapping Modrić and making his run into the box. The Croatian made a nice hesitation move, giving the impression that he might cut to the inside of the defender, before playing the ball wide to Vinícius Júnior.

The young Brazilian then cut inside on his right foot, engaged in a 1v1 battle with the keeper, and slipped the ball into the net. It proved to be the winning goal of the game, securing three big points in Real Madrid's title run.

Credit for the goal certainly belongs to Carvajal for the tackle and Vinícius Júnior for a fantastic overlapping run that started in the right half space. However, equal credit is due to Zidane. The team's rest defense allowed for a quick defensive transition. With Carvajal's quick recovery, Valverde and Modrić were able to use Mallorca's overcommitment in the counterattack against them.

*Chapter 5*

# The Glorious Return of Man-Marking

Improving the team's rest defense may have been Zidane's single most important tactical solution, but it wasn't the only defensive tactic he introduced to the side. Almost equally important is the return of man-marking in the high-press.

While most teams settled into their defensive structure in the early stages of the press, Zidane moved away from that idea, favoring man-marking in the high-press. It's a gamble that works well for physically and defensively dominant sides. Forwards and attacking midfielders get tight to the short and intermediate options, making it risky to play them. Defensive mids and the backline follow suit, typically ensuring they have one more defender along the backline than the opponent has attackers.

Long balls against excellent aerial defenders, as we see at Real Madrid, don't often work. That leaves teams scrambling to identify paths for ball progression.

From the defending team's point of view, the basic idea here was to force the opposition to start their attack from the deepest possible position. As Real Madrid gradually forced opponents to play negative passes in order to keep the ball, the opposition was simultaneously forced to start their attack from deep in their own half and had enough time to move into their more expansive attacking shape.

Despite the appearance of a positive, the trap was set.

*PPDA and the Counterpress*

When Real Madrid lost the ball, they counterpressed aggressively, but even that counterpress had its nuances. When most teams counterpress, the sole objective is to win the ball back as soon as possible.

## Real Madrid Passes Per Defensive Actions (PPDA)

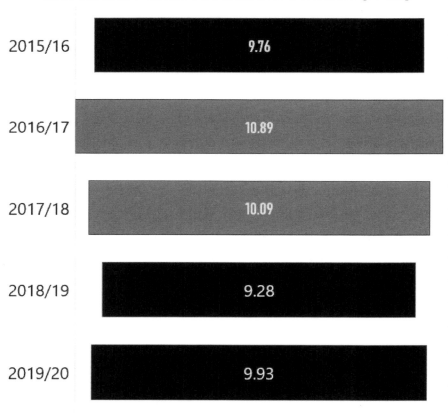

| Season | PPDA |
|--------|------|
| 2015/16 | 9.76 |
| 2016/17 | 10.89 |
| 2017/18 | 10.09 |
| 2018/19 | 9.28 |
| 2019/20 | 9.93 |

Let's put the counterpress in context.

For the season, Real Madrid registered a PPDA (passes per defensive action) of 9.93. What that means is that, in an average possession, Real Madrid's opponents completed 9.93 passes before Los Blancos recovered the ball. For context, PPDA below 10 indicates that the side is very aggressive in its pursuit of the ball and enjoys a great deal of success in recovering it. The higher the number, the greater a tendency a team has to sit back and absorb pressure, allowing the opposition to progress higher up the pitch before engaging.

In Real Madrid's case, the counterpress had two objectives: 1) to regain possession or 2) force the opponent backward.

That first point, regaining possession, is pretty straightforward. Teams with an aggressive counterpress often enjoy the lion's share of possession as well. They are teams whose playing philosophy requires dominance in possession, so a good counterpress is the quickest way to ensure the side regains the ball. More importantly, it also limits the effectiveness of the opponent's counterattack. Since possession-based teams tend to utilize expansive attacking shapes, the counterpress is designed to limit access to high targets.

That second point is closely tied to the second objective, which is forcing the opponents to play backward. Each time an opponent passes backward, also called a negative pass, it buys the pressing team precious seconds to recover their defensive shape.

As teams transition from an open possession into their defensive shape, the counterpress buys them time to get behind the ball and into their defensive starting points.

If the pressure defender was able to successfully force the first pass backward and his teammates, especially those within a 20-yard radius, were quick to pick up their defensive assignments in the man-marking high-press, opponents found it difficult to play forward with the second pass as well. If they were forced to play backward again, by that point, each Real Madrid player had usually picked up his nearest opponent.

Forcing the negative pass to set up the man-marking high-press was a non-negotiable in Zidane's defensive tactics. Ideally, their counterpressing would leave the opposition with one easy passing outlet, the goalkeeper. Madrid wanted their opponents to distribute from the deepest position possible. If not the goalie, they at least wanted one of the centerbacks orchestrating play.

From the deep starting point, opponents would find that Real Madrid used those seconds in the counterpress to man-mark any centrally located player, as well as all short and intermediate outlets. Further, the way man-marking was structured, Zidane ensured that his side was plus one at the back, meaning they had one more defender along the backline than the opposition had forwards. The only players left unmarked were the wingers. In order to play into those players, goalkeepers and centerbacks typically had to complete a 40 to 50-yard pass. Given the hang time of that pass and the fact that the nearest Real Madrid defender was only about 20 yards away, any long outlet pass into the wings was tightly contested.

Once Real Madrid had successfully transitioned into their man-marking high-press, the first step was accomplished. The second step involves the who and where.

The who is the player or players they want leading the attack. There are a few exceptions to this rule, but, in general, if you want any single player taking on playmaking responsibilities at the back, it's either the goalie or the weaker of the two centerbacks. Forcing one of those two players to act as the primary playmaker meant that Real Madrid was daring them to play over or through the high-press.

The only two players on the pitch that did not have a defender right on their back were the wide forwards or wide attacking mids. If the goalkeeper or weaker centerback played a pass to them from inside the box, then you're looking at a 40-yard flighted ball into the high and wide players. In the amount of time the ball would be in the air, Real Madrid could transition from a central superiority to cover the wings and contest the aerial pass.

With the forwards, midfielders, and outside-backs engaged in the man-marking high-press, opponents often tried to beat the Madrid press by winning the second ball. So, if a goalkeeper was responsible for distributing, he might try to hit his center forward with a long pass. That forward then tried to redirect the ball into the path of one of his teammates.

*Centerback Defensive Comparison*

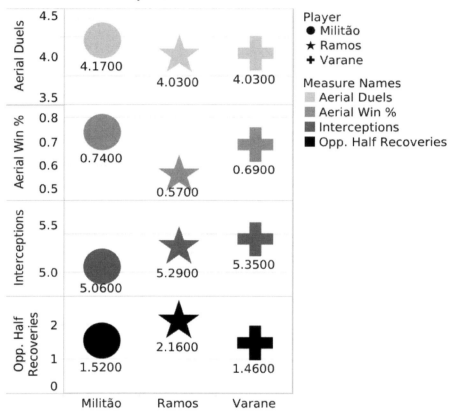

The issue, of course, is that this is easier said than done against Real Madrid. For one thing, Madrid's centerbacks were exceptional in the air. For the season, Militão won 74% of his aerial duels, Varane claimed 69%, and Sergio Ramos, the undersized centerback, emerged victorious in 57% of occasions.

Beyond the aerial duels, Real Madrid centerbacks, as well as Casemiro, were excellent at intercepting passes. When you think about it, it makes perfect sense. With the players higher up the pitch eliminating short and intermediate passing opportunities, the opponent was restricted in his options. Then, when his options are contextualized by the ecological dynamics of the game, you can reduce even more of his possible solutions. For example, if the goalkeeper has the ball on the right side of his six-yard box and his body orientation is directed towards the right side of the pitch, you can more or less eliminate the possibility of a long pass to his left outside-back or forward.

By reducing the number of possible targets, Casemiro and the backline were able to focus their attention on realistic possibilities. With those possibilities in mind, they improved their odds of intercepting the forward pass.

Another advantage of the man-marking high-press was the location of the recovery. With Casemiro and the centerbacks typically taking a conservative starting point, which was designed to prevent the opponent from playing into the space behind them, they were then able to move forward in recovery attempts. So, rather than recovering the ball in their defensive half of the pitch, they were instead able to accumulate a large number of opposition half recoveries.

*To the Drawing Board*

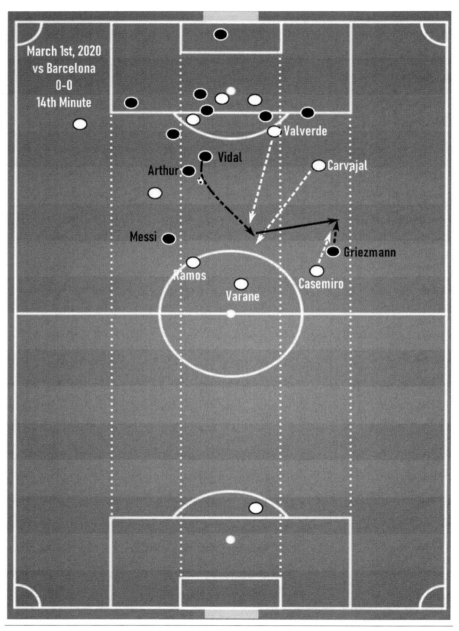

March 1st, 2020
vs Barcelona
0-0
14th Minute

Valverde

Vidal

Arthur

Carvajal

Messi

Griezmann

Ramos

Casemiro

Varane

This sequence in the second Clásico stands out. After a Kroos shot attempt ended in a loss of possession, Barcelona swarmed to the ball and tried to start a counterattack. Arthur got the first touch, then left the ball for the oncoming Arturo Vidal. As the Chilean dribbled forward, Carvajal used his half space starting point to good effect. He quickly closed Vidal's space, forcing him to abandon the dribble and play a negative pass to Antoine Griezmann.

It's important to note that this is just the counterpressing portion of Madrid's defensive engagement. As mentioned earlier one of the objectives in the counterpress is to force the opposition backward.

Though Real Madrid had three players behind the ball, Vidal's entry into the middle third gave Barcelona a 3v3 scenario. Plus, with Vidal running at Casemiro, he was attempting to pin the Brazilian to the spot, hoping to catch him flat-footed in order to play around him. With both Griezmann and Lionel Messi in front of him, playing around Casemiro would have sent Barcelona directly to goal.

But it wasn't meant to be.

In addition to Carvajal's pressure, Valverde was also nearby and ready to assist in the counterpress. The pressure of those two players left Vidal with no option but to abandon the dribble and play to his nearest target. Since Casemiro was poised to make the interception, the pass was played behind Griezmann, forcing him away from Casemiro to guarantee Barcelona kept possession of the ball.

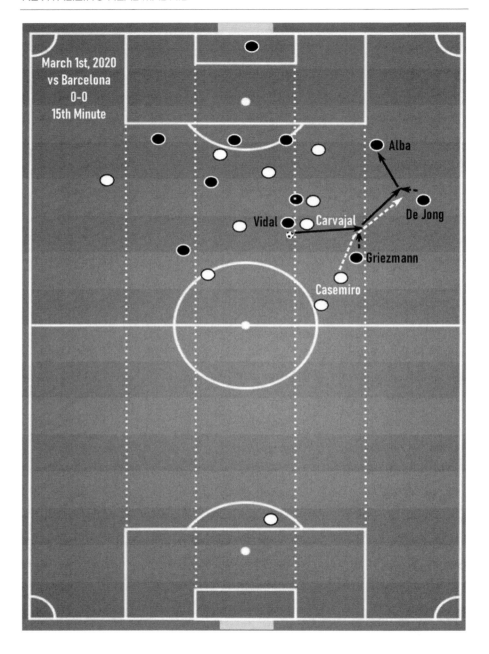

March 1st, 2020
vs Barcelona
0-0
15th Minute

Alba

De Jong

Vidal Carvajal

Griezmann

Casemiro

After an effective counterpress, Real Madrid transitioned to their next objective, which was forcing Barcelona to continue playing negative passes so that Madrid could set up the man-marking high-press. Although Jordi Alba was both deep and near the wings, Madrid wanted to push the build-out back even further.

After a sequence of passes between De Jong, Alba, and Griezmann, Real Madrid forced Barcelona to play in deeper and deeper areas in order to maintain possession of the ball.

Since they had already forced Barcelona into a series of negative passes, Madrid had bought time to establish the man-marking high-press. As you can see in the image, the only available short and intermediate-range passes were the ones to De Jong and Alba. All other Barcelona players were marked out of participation.

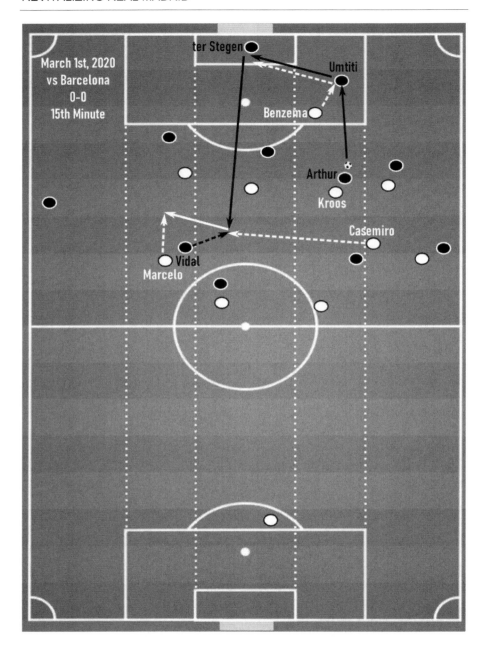

Without any forward options, Barcelona was resigned to starting attacks from deeper starting points.

Going into the game, Barcelona would gladly have accepted the challenge.

Marc-André ter Stegen is one of the best goalkeepers in the world with his technical ability and distributions. Allowing him to operate as a deep-lying playmaker seemed to suit Barcelona. With the ball at his feet, Barcelona could then pull Benzema or one of the other forwards out of the man-marking high-press, leaving one of the defenders open. ter Stegen could then play to his open teammate, initiating a chain reaction in Real Madrid's defense.

Though it worked on a couple of occasions, it didn't this time. As the sequence was nearing its end Arthur checked into the left half space and received a pass from Alba. With Real Madrid sending a player to mark Alba, Arthur was left with just one option, a pass back to Samuel Umtiti.

The issue with that pass is that Benzema was waiting for that specific pass. As Umtiti received the ball, he was immediately pressured by Benzema. Escaping through the dribble proved ineffective, but it did create a passing lane, as well as additional space cover for ter Stegen. Umtiti played back to his keeper who was again hurried by big Benz.

Without time on the ball or any open short and intermediate outlets, ter Stegen simply launched the ball forward.

Vidal moved centrally to try and claim the pass, but Casemiro was first to the ball. His anticipation and quick response time to ter Stegen's strike enabled him to arrive at the perfect time. With an aerial win, he was able to head the ball into the path of Marcelo. The high recovery ended with a shot for Real Madrid.

The reason I've chosen a single sequence to represent Real Madrid's counterpressing and man-marking high-press is because of how clear and effective it was. Though this tactic was employed throughout the season against both the top and bottom tier teams in La Liga, its effectiveness against Barcelona in the most important match of the season represents the tactical innovation and restructuring of this team.

*Why Did Man-Marking in the High-press Work?*

Entering the 2019/20 season, Zidane identified the team's defensive tactics as the main area for development. Without the guarantee of having two-plus goals per game, he had to restructure the team to ensure that they were more difficult to score against. In the end, it was Zidane's defensive tactics that revitalized the team. Knowing that his side would still struggle to score goals, especially once Hazard appeared at camp overweight, then picked up one injury after another, he knew he could recreate this team into a defensive juggernaut. All the pieces of the puzzle were there, he just had to find the right fit.

Man-marking in a high-press worked so well for a number of reasons.

First, there was a team-wide commitment to pressing. When the forwards and attacking midfielders buy into the extra defensive work, they limit the opponent's channels of progression. By limiting those attacking options, the deeper players have to account for fewer variables. Simplifying the game worked wonders for this Madrid side.

Second, Madrid's superior athletes produced quick defensive transitions and harassed the opposition ball-carriers.

Finally, the opponent was left with long diagonals, which were easy to contest, or playing into the pack of Casemiro, Ramos, and Varane.

Some opponents reached the point where they simply hit the long ball and let Real Madrid restart possession. They didn't expect to beat the press anyway, so why not reduce risk in the build-up and play for another counterattack.

Teams went into these games knowing opportunities would be sparse. They had to patiently await the right chance, then fully invest in it when the timing was right. When they managed to get into the box, there was a big Belgian waiting for them too.

## Chapter 6

# Thibaut Courtois: A World-Class Season

With Courtois and Navas splitting time in net during the 2018/19 season, there was an odd tension between the two players, the club, and the supporters. One of the club's most influential players over the previous few seasons, Navas was a hero among the fans and widely supported by his teammates. It's not necessarily that he was viewed as more talented than Courtois, but there was a sense that Navas' performance levels hadn't dropped off, so casting him aside reeked of injustice.

Courtois' early struggles and Navas' presence led to a nightmare season for the Belgian international. Whistled at home, in and out of the lineup, and struggling to adapt to a new playing style, his first season at the club fell well short of expectations. Shaky with the ball at his feet and conceding the occasional soft goal, there was a call for Navas to hold the starting goalkeeping role.

Despite Courtois' struggles, Zidane pushed forward with the transfer of Navas, handing Courtois the full-time role. Moving the popular Costa Rican to PSG accomplished that objective and brought in a reliable backup as well.

With Navas out of the equation, Courtois looked like a new man during the 2019/20 campaign. Sure, Real Madrid's improved defense helped him tremendously, but even though the volume of shots against was down, Courtois still had to contend with the high-quality shots possession-oriented teams tend to concede.

During his Atlético Madrid and Chelsea days, the big Belgian established himself as one of the top shot-stoppers in the world. It's the quality that made him most appealing in the eyes of Florentino Pérez.

However, when you're looking at the other teams on his resume, they simply didn't have comparable attacking philosophies to Real Madrid. With Los Blancos, Courtois was expected to use his feet and use them well. His second season with the club showed marked improvement in that area. He became a reliable partner during the build-up and the defenders showed more confidence in him as well.

*Courtois' Season in Numbers*

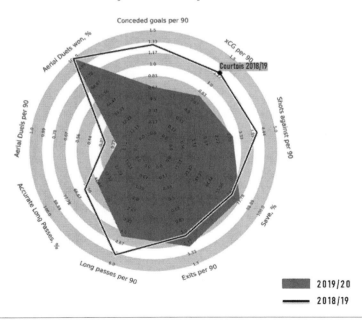

The decision to hand Courtois the full-time job paid off handsomely. This radar compares Courtois' 2019/20 and 2018/19 seasons. In nearly every category, his second season with the club is far superior to his first.

Much maligned for his poor feet, he sent more long passes per 90 minutes in his second season and improved his accuracy in that category. In his second season at the club, you see that he was more than just a shot-stopper. He had become the complete goalkeeper, much like Navas and Iker Casillas before him.

His save percentage declined, but he also faced fewer shots per game and nearly halved the number of goals he conceded per 90. With a greater percentage of low-quality shots off the table, his save percentage was bound to regress.

In 34 La Liga games, Courtois played 3276 minutes and conceded just 20 goals. That comes out to 0.55 goals against P90. Compare that total to his first season at the club. During the 2018/19 campaign, the Belgian played 2569 minutes. While in net, the team allowed 36 goals, a 1.26 average per game.

Those are the concrete stats about balls that ended up in the back of the net, but what about expected goals?

On the radar, you'll see the xCG per 90 stat. That measures how many goals a keeper should reasonably have been expected to concede in a given game.

In 2018/19, Courtois had an xCG P90 of 1.16. When held in contrast to the actual number of goals he conceded, the former Chelsea man allowed 0.10

more goals per game than an average goalkeeper would have conceded with those same shots.

Fast-forward to 2019/20, after he had a year to adapt to the club, Real Madrid's playing philosophy, and was the clear #1 in goal, the numbers show his tremendous improvement. For the season, his xCG per 90 was 0.67, which is itself a credit to Zidane's incredible tactical adjustments. Courtois managed to beat that xCG P90 mark with his 0.55 goals against average.

From one season to the next, he went from a -0.10 discrepancy between goals against P90 and expected conceded goal P90 to a +0.12 mark. That's a +0.22 swing.

Trying to account for the improved performance is challenging since there are several factors to consider, but you have to assume the adaptation period and moving into the clear #1 role were major factors. It's also interesting to note the improvement while dealing with fewer shots against. Though conceding large volumes of shots is typically a team-wide negative, at least before considering shooting locations, many goalkeepers will argue that facing more shots allows for a better flow in performance. For possession heavy teams like Real Madrid, long spells of possession and excellent pressing higher up the pitch limit the keeper's activity. To have this type of improvement in a season that saw him face 29% fewer shots per game is all the more impressive.

*Feet are for More Than Just Standing*

One of the ways possession-dominate teams can help a goalie stay mentally active is by incorporating him in the attacking phases. Courtois struggled in this area during his first season at the club, but his progress in this area is undeniable.

As Madrid faced compact middle blocks, feeling an increase in pressure with each pass, Courtois' teammates used him as a means of recycling play, getting a fresh start with the long pass back. Playing into Courtois allowed the team to regain their attacking shape and restart the build-out.

Another area where he proved reliable was as the pressure release valve when the team went up against a high-press. Even with the limited time and space players experience in an opponent's high-press, Courtois proved that he was a reliable deep option. And it's not as though he was the last possible option. During the 2019/20 season, it was clear his teammates regarded him as a valuable contributor to the team's build-out.

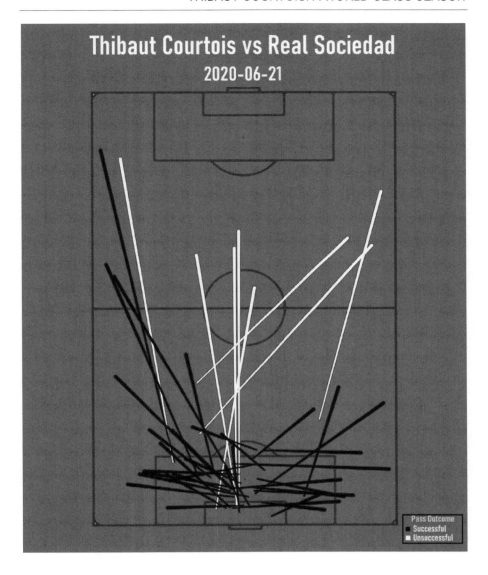

To give an idea of his long passing contribution, we can look at an example from June 21st, 2020 against Real Sociedad. In this match, in particular, we have a nice balance of high usage passing and a variety of passing distances. There's a clear preference to play to the left side of the pitch, which makes sense given that he's a left-footed player. There's also the fact that Ramos and

Kroos, the team's two most important players in the build-up, play on the left-hand side of the pitch.

When Courtois plays into the center and right regions of the pitch, the drop in accuracy is noticeable, at least in situations when he's playing a long-range pass. If the distance falls into the short or intermediate categories, he's equally confident playing to any part of the field.

You could argue that, for a guy who's known primarily as a shot-stopping goalkeeper, even average distribution ability would be the cherry on top. However, for a club like Real Madrid, a ball-playing keeper is a necessity.

Since Real Madrid is a possession dominant team, the goalie plays an integral role as the team builds out of the back. He's also the release valve if the opposition's high-press or middle block puts his teammates under duress. That deep outlet can mean the difference between a low turnover or breaking the opposition's press and igniting a direct attack on their goal.

Year number two was much more positive in that regard. Courtois has exceptional range with his distributions, so it was always just a matter of incorporating those distributions within the flow of the game or improving his ability to hit the long target.

Courtois not only showed that he's reliable with the ball at his feet, but he also earned the Zamora Trophy, which the Spanish newspaper MARCA gives to the goalkeeper who has the lowest "goals-to-game" ratio. It was his third Zamora overall, first with Real Madrid.

Courtois' performances in net were certainly a major contributor to the team's success, but he's not the only player at the back who improved under Zidane. His radar shows the extraordinary drop in shots against, which is a testament to Zidane's tactical developments that we've already addressed, but we also have to look at the individual player performances across the pitch.

With the exception of Ferland Mendy, who split time with Marcelo at left-back, the backline and midfield were largely unchanged from one season to the next. It's difficult to look beyond the centerback pairing, especially the career year from Sergio Ramos.

## Chapter 7

# The Ramos and Varane Partnership

The backbone of Real Madrid's improved performances in the 2019/20 campaign was the club's improved defensive tactics. The man-marking high-press was certainly influential, but a lot of credit goes to the way the backline operated.

2018/19 was a difficult year for the centerbacks. At times, it was difficult watching games and seeing opponents pick apart the Real Madrid press. As the opposition transitioned to the counterattack, I'd venture to say many Madridistas simultaneously expressed the same thoughts, be it vocally or mentally. In fact, the thought process looked pretty similar to the seven stages of grief.

When opponents gained possession of the ball, the first thought went something like, "OH MY GOSH WE'RE NOT READY FOR THIS." Shock.

Second, there was denial: "We'll be okay, Casemiro, Ramos, and Varane will end the counterattack. We're good."

As opponents played around Casemiro and pulled Ramos into midfield, the third stage, anger, made an appearance: "IT'S THE SAME PATTERN EVERY TIME! WHY DON'T THEY SEE IT?"

Next up, bargaining: "Please Courtois/Navas, I know we ask a lot from you, but, please, save us."

Once an opponent scored, depression set in: "This is our season. If you need me, I'll be busy abandoning all hope."

Testing followed. That's where the super-fan drew out his solutions, pinning them across the wall and connecting them with a string like he's the Sherlock Holmes of the soccer universe.

Finally, acceptance: "We're broken. I miss Zidane and Ronaldo. Please come back and fix us."

No Ronaldo, at least not yet, but Zidane did return, bringing tactical solutions with him.

We covered the central square and man-marking high-press. Those were the major tactical advancements that changed the club's fortunes.

It changed the fortunes of the centerbacks as well. 2018/19 saw the doubters come out in force, arguing that Ramos was past his prime and a successor was needed. Turns out he and Varane only needed more help from the team's tactics.

*Setting the Centerbacks up for Success*

As the attackers engaged higher up the pitch, be it in a counterpress or simply in a high-press, the coverage at the back was critical for Real Madrid's success.

We often saw the side plus one at the back, meaning they had one more defender than the opposition had attackers. Typically either Ramos or Varane filled that role as the number up defender. To give them protection and ensure that the opposition could not run at the backline, therefore destroying the plus one advantage Zidane wanted, Casemiro filled the role just in front of the two centerbacks. The Brazilian was the muscle in the midfield, using his physicality, anticipation, and recognition of play to rate among the league leaders in interceptions once again with 7.19 per 90 minutes.

Even with improved coverage in front of the line, there was still work to be done for Ramos and Varane. In the previous season, when the team was engaged in a high-press, Real Madrid's backline had a tendency to become disjointed, with Ramos, and occasionally Varane as well, moving too high into the midfield, leaving massive gaps behind them. Though Varane is rarely beaten for pace, if he is caught out and the opposition allowed to run behind him, even the Frenchman's recovery speed doesn't guarantee safety. The previous season, when Real Madrid was caught on the break, we often saw one of the two centerbacks catch the first attacker (the ball carrier), but it was always the second attacker who was the likely goal-scoring threat. With the team engaged so high up the pitch, recoveries were difficult to manage.

*The Importance of Defensive Tactics*

In 2019/20, defensive engagements were more responsive than reactive.

What's the difference?

During Zidane's gap year, the team's tactics revolved primarily around the attacking phases of the game, particularly connecting the lines and discovering avenues for the final pass. With most opponents willing to get everyone behind the ball and deny easy progress through the middle of the field, Real simply committed more numbers forward.

To an extent, this is a logical decision. As opponents drop numbers behind the ball, there's less of a risk higher up the pitch. The decreased risk in the middle third of the field then allows a team to move more attackers higher up the pitch. In fact, if the opponent has 10 or 11 players behind the ball, it's necessary to push your numbers higher into more threatening positions.

The issue that arises is when the balance of attacking and defensive tactics is thrown off-kilter. Gauging that relationship is difficult, especially in a dynamic sport like soccer. With the ecological dynamics (context of the game) constantly changing, players have to discover how their team's tactical approach can solve the ever-changing problems presented by the opposition. New angles, different looks, and superiorities in key areas all factor into the player's decision-making process.

With Madrid overcompensating with their attacking tactics, the strain on the three deepest players increased.

Ask any scout or analyst if it's difficult to assess a centerback and, aside from easily deciphered physical abilities, you'll hear that they're the toughest group to analyze. Whereas the attacking stats offer easier comparisons due to their proactive nature, much of a backline's defensive statistics depend on what's happening higher up the pitch.

For example, it's fair to say Ramos and Varane performed at a higher level in 2019/20 than the year beforehand. However, the comparison is weakened by the fact that the team's tactics, especially in the way they protected the centerbacks, was much improved.

2018/19 forced Ramos and Varane to scramble into their defensive duties. It was pure chaos, largely due to the ease in which opponents accessed the backline.

From a defensive standpoint, the goal is to limit the number of options an opponent has, which, in turn, refines the attention of the defending players. As options are narrowed, a team will then look to determine where an opponent can go and when they can make the move. If the where and when are determined, the defensive response is incredibly simplified. Fewer possibilities lead to a better response and chance of success.

Better pressing higher up the pitch gave the centerbacks the protection they needed. With fewer risks to assess, they could focus on doing specific actions well rather than covering an 80x80 yard area.

*Attacking Involvement*

Improving the defensive tactics carried the added benefit of creating more routine attacking contributions.

From a statistical standpoint, the centerbacks were less active during the 2019/20 season as compared to 2018/19.

One reason is that Real Madrid spent less time butting heads with the low block. The Lopetegui side in particular spent far too much time trying to break the wall of opponents 30 yards from goal. His response was to use Ramos and Varane as deep-lying playmakers. With their passing range and positioning outside of the opposition's press, they had the time and space to play over and around the block.

While they fulfilled their duties, the defending team's compact shape proved difficult to break.

Moving forward to 2019/20, the team still encountered the low block, but they spent less time doing so. By dropping Kroos into a deeper part of the field, he, Ramos, and Varane constructed the build-up to determine the point of engagement. Madrid didn't want to allow the opposition to set their line of confrontation (where they start pressuring the ball) 30 yards from goal.

Instead, Los Blancos used the middle third to move from "preparing to attack the opponent" to "attacking the opponent." In doing so, the centerbacks joined Kroos as the deep-lying playmakers, using long, diagonal distributions to play over the opposition's middle block.

# Centerback Passing Stats

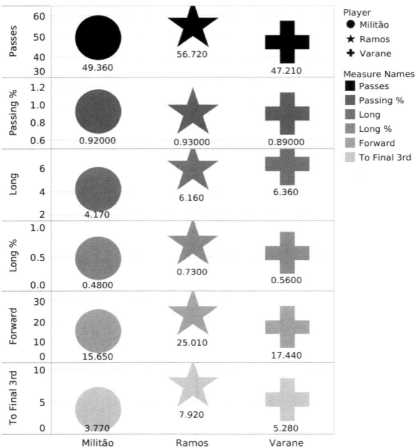

Looking at the centerback statistics from 2019/20, Ramos' influence is undeniable. Leading the group in all but the long passes P90 category, the team looked to him as a deep creator. His 56.72 passes P90 and 25.01 forward passes P90 are especially significant. Those stats, especially when held in comparison to Varane and Militão, show how significant he was to Real Madrid's attacking tactics. More than an aggressive, ball-winning centerback, he is also one of the best on-the-ball central defenders in the world.

Varane isn't too far off the mark either. Though Ramos beats him in most volume and efficiency categories, the Frenchman has proven more than capable of breaking lines. With Kroos and Ramos serving as the focal points of the build-out, Varane does well to locate spaces that allow him to receive the ball from the left and play forward through the right. His starting point and body orientation allow him to quickly connect the actions of receiving and passing.

Militão, who was in his first year with the club at the ripe old age of 21 (turned 22 in January 2020), was some ways off in several of the categories, but this is a case of needing patience with a young player. Keep in mind that centerbacks, like 34-year-old Sergio Ramos, tend to peak later in their careers. Since it's primarily a response-heavy job, it takes time to improve pattern recognition and risk assessment. Add in that it was his first season in a new country and playing philosophy and the lower totals are understandable.

*To the Drawing Board*

Defensive tactics and the roles of the centerbacks have received extensive coverage thus far. And you know what, they should. Given the side's attacking inconsistencies, it was the defensive work that secured the title.

That said, these tactical images will mostly focus on the attacking side of the game. There's an image about Ramos' improved movements into midfield, but we want to look at build-out and set piece contributions as well.

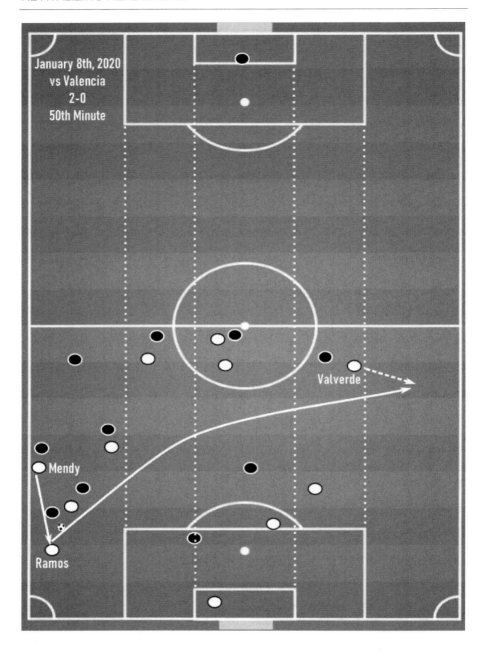

January 8th, 2020
vs Valencia
2-0
50th Minute

Valverde

Mendy

Ramos

During the side's January match-up against Valencia, Real Madrid found themselves pinned deep in their own end of the field with Valencia man for man in a high-press. Both Kroos and Casemiro slid over to help the build-out, but their paths to the ball were blocked by Valencia players. With Mendy in possession of the ball and facing his own goal, a negative pass to Sergio Ramos was the most realistic, as well as the safest, means of breaking the press.

Mendy played back to Ramos who took his first touch across his body to set up his right foot. With Valencia unbalanced to Real Madrid's left, the captain picked out Federico Valverde, who was isolated with a defender near midfield on the far side of the pitch.

That first touch allowed Ramos to go immediately into his long diagonal distribution. To ensure the pass was uncontested, he played the ball roughly 10 yards behind Valverde near the touchline. You see, Valencia is a team that prioritizes the counterattack, especially against a possession dominant team like Real Madrid. Had Ramos hung a contested ball for Valverde, he would have increased the likelihood of Valencia winning the aerial duel, claiming the second ball, and running into wide open space on Real Madrid's right-hand side.

By playing the ball 10 yards behind Valverde and forcing the Uruguayan to move closer to the sideline, Ramos was effectively calculating the odds of an aerial duel while also acknowledging his team's vulnerability on the right. Since he played the ball in a spot where only Valverde could claim that long diagonal pass, he safeguarded Madrid against the possible Valencia counterattack.

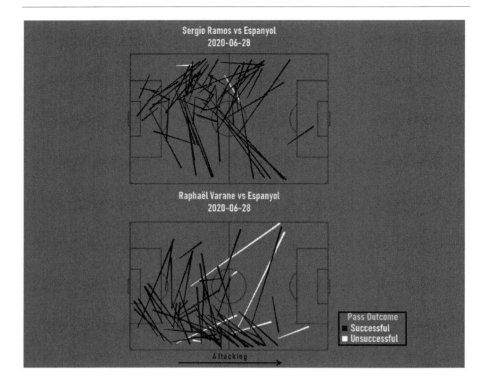

In this image, we have Sergio Ramos and Raphaël Varane's pass map from their June match-up against Espanyol.

A couple of things worth noting are the distances of the passes and the point of origin.

Both centerbacks are comfortable and confident playing over the opposition's defense, sending long diagonals to the opposite side of the pitch. Between the two centerbacks and Kroos, Real Madrid have three players who can progress the ball from deep areas during the build-up phase.

In addition to half space starting points deep in their own half, you can see that Varane and Ramos are both influential once the team enters the attacking half of the field.

As Real Madrid entered the final third, it was common to see opponents move into a low block. As the opponent moved 9 or 10 players behind the ball, the central channel and half spaces became very compact. When opponents overloaded in the central portion of the pitch, Los Blancos would freely swing the ball from one wing to the other.

However, recycling the ball from one wing to the other doesn't offer much help in penetrating the low block. Yes, the block slides horizontally, but it maintains its vertical compaction. That's where Varane and Ramos joined Kroos and Modrić as attacking third playmakers.

It's important to note that Ramos' runs into the box would not be possible without his passing range and accuracy. Because he is able to serve the team as a passer who breaks the low block, he routinely looks for pockets of space higher up the pitch. As opposing forwards drop behind the ball, you'll see Ramos looking for opportunities to jump in line with Toni Kroos while also securing his side against the opposition's counterattack. As opponents drop deeper Ramos can afford to move higher, especially if Kroos and one of the other two midfielders maintain deeper positions.

Ramos in particular is well known for his bursts into midfield. Before he sprints forward to meet a cross, you will commonly see him pushing higher up the pitch in very gradual steps. If the opponent is sitting in a low block, he'll look for pockets of space in the left half space or central channel. If he can receive there, he'll decide whether to pass or dribble at the opposition's block before sending the ball into one of the two wings. If the latter, once he releases the pass and limits the space the other team can run into, Ramos transitions from a pass-oriented playmaker to an aerial threat in the box.

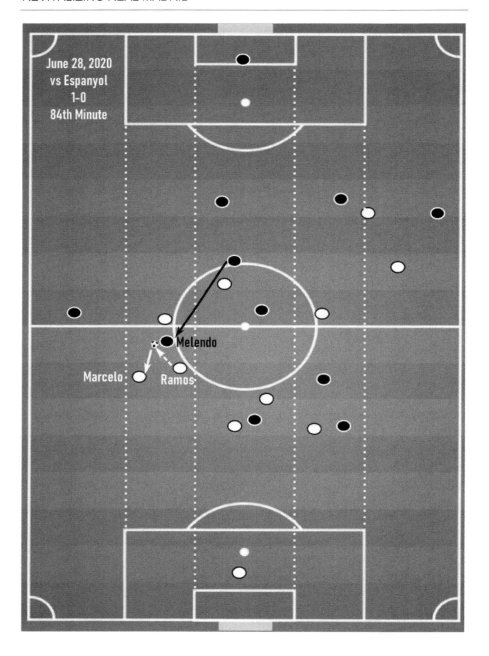

During the 2018/19 season, Ramos' abandonment of depth to move into midfield and pressure ball carriers was a major source of concern for the team. With Varane left to cover the full width of the pitch behind him, Real Madrid was routinely carved up in the counterattack.

We still saw Ramos make those aggressive moves into midfield during the 2019/20 campaign, but the manner in which he engaged had changed. To contextualize his movements into midfield, those forward runs typically fall into one of two categories. First, there was a near guarantee that he would win the ball. If he didn't win it, he would at least foul the opponent to kill the threat.

Second, he made sure there was coverage around him. You'll recall an earlier sequence in which Ramos aggressively stepped into midfield while Marcelo was caught behind his mark. As Ramos stepped up, the opposition simply played into the space behind Ramos.

Late in the team's June match-up against Espanyol, we saw Ramos move aggressively into midfield with both conditions in place. Not only did he have coverage from Mendy, but he also had a great step on Melendo and very high odds of completing the tackle. With the two assurances in place, Ramos confidently stepped forward and won the ball for his side.

It must be said that Marcelo showed a greater commitment to the team's defensive tactics, but it's also worth noting how much of an impact Ferland Mendy had on this aspect of the game. While the Frenchman will never offer the explosive attacking ability of prime Marcelo, Mendy's pace and stamina allowed him to offer more consistent two-way play than Marcelo. As opponents looked to counterattack against Real Madrid, Mendy dutifully recovered his ground to protect his side against the threat.

With the left-backs offering a greater presence in both the counterpress and the team's recovery, the variables Ramos had to calculate decreased, allowing him to be more decisive with his movements into midfield. And again, when he did go, he had the support of his teammates. Beyond the presence of Varane, we saw the left-back, Casemiro, and Kroos offered better coverage in 2019/20 than they had the previous season.

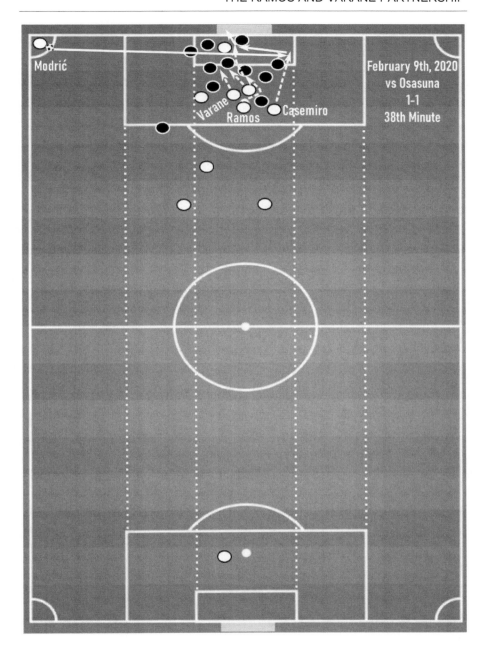

The final aspect of the Ramos/Varane partnership to discuss is the way Zidane used the two players in set piece situations. As the team's two best aerial threats, Zidane looked to put his two centerbacks in connection with each other, especially during corner kicks.

Ramos and Varane typically played off each other, one looking to free the other for a run into the box. Whether it was by setting a pick or one carving out a path for the other to run into, the two players were the focal point of Real Madrid set pieces.

In the image, we see Modrić taking a corner kick while Ramos and Varane looked to time their runs from the top of the box. Varane led the way, making the first run into the box while Ramos ran directly behind him. With Varane running at Ramos' mark and drawing his own to the near post as well, the Frenchman's movement prevented Osasuna from getting tight to Ramos.

As a cross sailed over their heads to the far post, Casemiro managed to head the ball back across the box, right into the path of Ramos. Since the captain was freed by Varane's run, he was left unmarked at the near post, easily heading the ball into the back of the net.

Ramos and Varane have been one of the game's best centerback pairings in recent years. One of the reasons is due to their complementary playing styles and skillsets. Another is that the chemistry has developed to such a point that each has very clear and defined roles. With each having a clear understanding of what he expects from the other and how to play off of their strengths and weaknesses, they have leveraged each other's talents to form a formidable central presence.

That presence is felt on both sides of the ball. In the attack, each is press resistant, capable of playing through the opponent's defensive structure, be it in a high-press, middle block, or low block. Though Varane's long-range passing doesn't have quite the reputation of Ramos', he's equally capable of breaking an opponent's structure with a long-range pass.

Defensively, the aggression and physicality of Ramos pieced perfectly with Varane's pace and coverage instincts. When you have a centerback who moves forward as aggressively as Ramos does, a more conservative partner who prioritizes coverage is essential. That's where this partnership has worked out brilliantly. Varane's pace and coverage instincts pair perfectly with Ramos' aggressive, physical approach.

To this point, the book has focused almost exclusively on Zidane's defensive tactics, both in open play and transition.

Even though attacking numbers were down again in 2019/20, this is still Real Madrid. Down by their standards, they were still among the league leaders in goals scored and xG.

It all starts at the back with a well-constructed build-up, which is our next stop.

*Chapter 8*

# Preparing to Attack the Opponent

It's strange to think a Real Madrid book can wait until nearly the middle of the book to present the current season's attacking solutions, but that's where we find ourselves. And, in a sense, it's a perfect fit for 2020.

It may have been the strangest season in league history. The Spanish Civil War led to canceled seasons from 1936 to 1939, but, beyond those years, La Liga hadn't seen a year like 2019/20.

Coming into the season, Real Madrid had hoped 2018/19 would be the anomaly. With Eden Hazard becoming the latest Galáctico to enter the fray, an exciting young forward in Luka Jović, and reinforcements across the pitch, the offseason offered hope that the goals would return to Real Madrid.

Once again, we must emphasize that, in 2020, there was no such thing as normal.

Injuries throughout the pitch, including to the new superstar, Hazard, as well as the talented young Marco Asensio, left Zidane scrambling to piece together his lineups.

It's not just a matter of putting quality players on the pitch together. He had those in abundance. The concern was fitting the right pieces of the puzzle together, leveraging players' skill sets became challenging as the number of possible combinations decreased. Remember, one of the superiorities is socio-affective, which considers the relationships between players on the pitch. Players who work well off of each other can create socio-affective superiorities. The opponents might not have qualitative advantages, but they can use socio-affective superiorities against Real Madrid's makeshift lineups.

Since Zidane believes in rotations anyway, the injuries just made his job a little bit tougher. While he does value the flow that consecutive starts generate, especially with a stable, preferred starting XI, he's a big believer in rotating the squad in order to keep them fit. Ironically, it's the fitness levels that caused greater rotation.

That's where the philosophy and identity brought on by Zidane's return to the club was so important.

One area where the club looked more fluid under Zidane was in the build-out phase, which you can also term as preparing to attack the opponents.

An effective build-out gave the players time to gain their attacking shape, which was especially important for the more advanced players. As they dropped deeper and pinched in to help defend against the opposition's attack or, in the case of long balls played into the feet of Courtois, transitioning from their man-marking duties into the team's positional play, the build-out bought time for the highest players to transition into the next phase of play.

If the opponent was using a high-press, building out of the back served not only to get Real Madrid into their attacking shape, but also to start manipulating the shape of the opposing defense. Through vertical and horizontal passing with coordinated movements from the midfielders and forwards, Real Madrid could create imbalances in the opposition's defense while also generating superiorities higher up the pitch.

A major difference between preparing to attack a high-press as opposed to a middle block is that the transition from preparing to attack the opponents to then attacking them is on an expedited itinerary. With little time and space to construct the attack, ensuring numeric superiority around the ball, drawing the opposition in to unbalance their shape, and then playing out of pressure occurs within a smaller time frame. But, with the opposition fully committing to pressuring the ball carrier, vulnerabilities emerge between the makeshift pressing lines.

When up against a high-press, it was common to see Real Madrid drop their most press resistant players into the defensive third to first, help recover the ball, but then to also play out of the opponent's counterpress. Once the counterpress was over, if the opponent continued to high-press, players like Luka Modrić and Isco might drop in to help the team play out of pressure.

For teams preferring the middle block, the build-out started higher up the pitch. With more time built into that transition from a compact defensive structure into the team's more expansive attacking shape, the transition between starting points occurred at a slower pace. In a sense, it was a calm before the storm, a brief period to recover some energy before reigniting the attack.

From a middle block, the preference is for structure over pressure. Middle block teams might set pressing traps, trying to force the opponents to play into specific areas of the midfield before collapsing on the ball carrier. They might also take away the central channel and half spaces, daring their opponent to play over or around them. If middle block teams funnel play into the wings, they can then shift their defense towards the ball, defending in three of the five channels with the two far-sided channels left unoccupied. In doing so, they can squeeze the spaces around the ball and attempt to force a bad pass from the opposition.

Against middle blocks, Los Merengues could afford to be more deliberate with their preferred build-out personnel and starting points.

*Real Madrid's Response to the Press*

With Toni Kroos, Sergio Ramos, and Raphaël Varane on the team, beating the high-press or breaking through a middle block isn't a big ask. Known for their distribution qualities, they could handle the limited time and space of high-pressing opponents and were perhaps even more comfortable against the middle block. When opponents drop into the middle third of the pitch, they concede the right to impact the deep distributors' starting points.

With those three orchestrating the build-out from the back, the players higher up the pitch moved into their starting points. Each team has their own set of positional responsibilities. For Real Madrid, there was more fluidity to their positional play than most teams. That's in large part due to the fact that, like Europe's other elites, they benefit from having supremely talented players in their squad.

Another influence in creating a more fluid playing style is that they more frequently encounter rigid defenses. Since the opponents are well-structured, tightening spaces between the lines and limiting access to the central region of the pitch, Madrid have to incorporate additional movements and player rotations to generate superiorities and unbalanced opponents during periods of extreme focus and organization.

To facilitate the attack upon the opponent, it's common to see Real Madrid's forwards and midfielders connecting with each other higher up the pitch. The outside-backs will also move higher. If they receive the ball, the team will either look for progression around the opposition's lines or to draw the opponent to one wing before switching the point of attack to the other.

*To the Drawing Board*

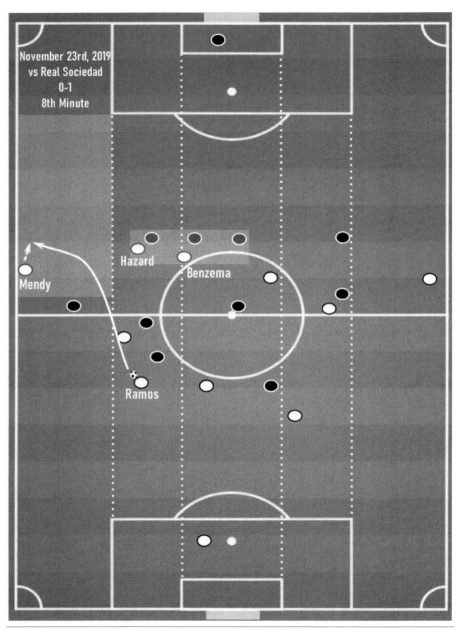

November 23rd, 2019
vs Real Sociedad
0-1
8th Minute

Hazard

Benzema

Mendy

Ramos

The November matchup against Real Sociedad saw Real Madrid setting up an attack against the middle block. Ramos had possession of the ball in the left half space with Kroos just in front of him, Casemiro occupying the central channel, and Varane offering a deep option in the right half space.

Elsewhere on the pitch, Mendy and Carvajal moved high up the formation, offering width. In order to secure the buildup, the forwards and midfielders were stationed from half space to half space. Hazard was situated in the left half space with Benzema at the edge of the central channel with Modrić and Rodrygo occupying similar spaces on the right.

Ramos and Kroos were in their left half space hotspots directing the possession.

In the sequence, it was the four deepest players who were responsible for initiating the attack. Ramos and Kroos were the two players most likely to play forward with Varane offering a deep outlet and Casemiro featuring as more of a bounce pass option.

One of the keys in this build-out was the positioning of Hazard and Benzema. With those two players tucked inside, they managed to occupy three of the four backline members. The fourth was the left-back, Nacho Monreal. Hazard's half space positioning left Mendy with unrestricted access to the wing. Once Portu shifted his focus from Mendy to the ball, Real Madrid's left-back made his move of the left-wing.

Ramos picked up the run and played a lofted ball into Mendy's path.

Between those four deep players and Courtois, Real Madrid had enough numbers around the ball to launch the attack plus the deep outlet if needed.

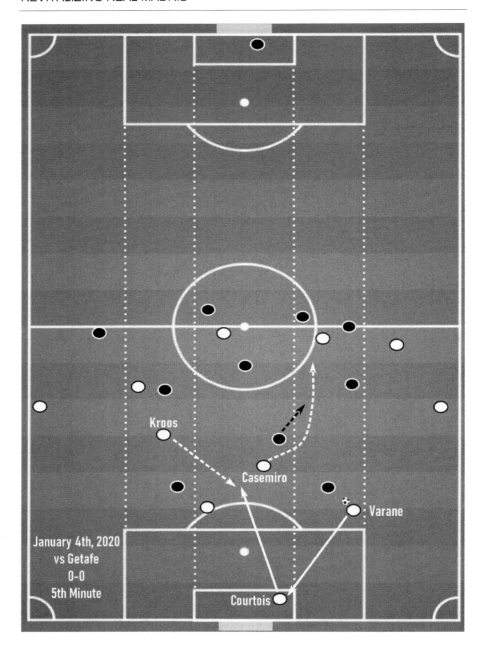

January 4th, 2020
vs Getafe
0-0
5th Minute

Against clubs with an aggressive and effective high-press, it was common to see Casemiro move higher up the pitch.

The move served a few purposes.

First, as the least press-resistant player of the four, Casemiro moved higher up the pitch in order to minimize the chances of a mistake. With Real Madrid in their build-out structure, a lost ball in the defensive third would, at the very least, end with the opponents having a crack at goal. Moving Casemiro higher up the pitch lets Kroos, Ramos, and Varane, who are more comfortable with the ball at their feet, direct the build-out.

The second reason for Casemiro leaving his deep position is that he pulls an opponent away from the press. With fewer opponents congesting Real Madrid's defensive third, Los Blancos could circulate the ball more freely, reducing the opponent's chances of intercepting the ball.

Finally, as Casemiro leaves, Kroos then moves into that central space. In this sequence against Getafe, Casemiro moved higher up the pitch while Varane played the ball back to Courtois. At that same time, Kroos was moving from the left half space into the central channel, right into the space Casemiro vacated.

With Getafe committing one player in their press to both Kroos and Isco, the German's run was untracked, allowing Real Madrid to break the first line of the press and start their move up the field.

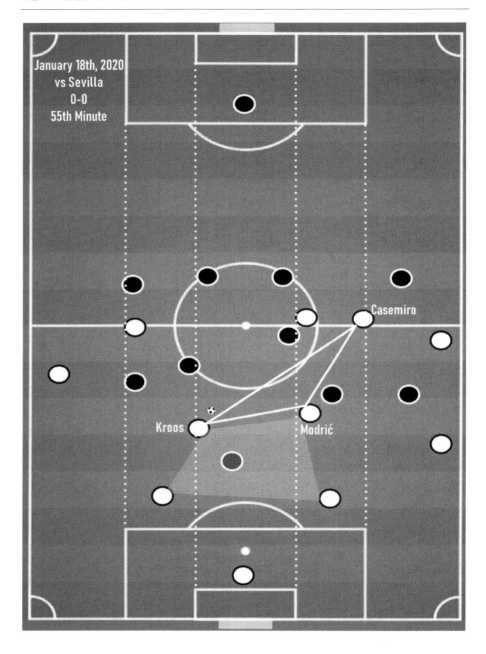

January 18th, 2020
vs Sevilla
0-0
55th Minute

Casemiro

Kroos

Modrić

When Casemiro, Kroos, and Modrić formed the midfield triumvirate, another common tactic in the buildup was to have Casemiro leave his deep position, switching roles with Luka Modrić.

Much like the last build-out pattern, which emphasized press resistance, this approach allowed Real Madrid to play Modrić and allow him to use his press resistance, vision, and distribution from a deeper area.

When Los Blancos applied this tactic, much like they did against a high-pressing Sevilla team in January of 2020, the four players formed a quadrilateral in the center of the pitch. The two centerbacks pinched a little wider into the half spaces, but the basic idea was to get four press resistant players to lead the build-out.

The added advantage is found in Casemiro's high positioning. Real Madrid were among the league leaders and crosses sent per game, but a common issue was a lack of suitable aerial targets in the box. With Casemiro higher up the pitch, progression into the final third put less pressure on a creative penalty box entry.

With both Casemiro and Benzema in the box, Real Madrid then had two aerial threats to contest crosses.

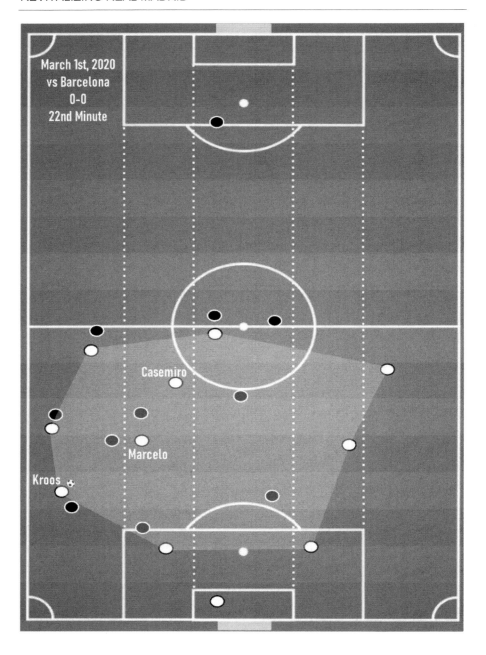

March 1st, 2020
vs Barcelona
0-0
22nd Minute

Casemiro

Marcelo

Kroos

The final build-out pattern we'll address is the wide overload.

An example of this pattern came in El Clasico. With La Blaugrana committed to a high-press, Real Madrid funneled the build-out through Kroos on the left side of the field.

Between Kroos and his teammates, six Real Madrid players occupied either the left-wing or the left half space. That left Benzema as the lone player in the central channel, Varane and Carvajal in the right half space, and Valverde in the right-wing.

Looking at the image, the shaded area shows only Marcelo and Casemiro playing within the team's attacking shape. There's a clear emphasis on attacking through the wings, especially on the left-hand side.

One advantage of the wing overload is that the build-out occurs away from the middle of the pitch. If the press is successful and wins the ball, the transition to goal is more direct from the central channel.

By initiating the attack in the wings, Real Madrid elongated the distance from their goal.

Additionally, playing into the wing has caused Barcelona to become unbalanced on the left side of the pitch. From Kroos' positioning on the ball, he has a number of options, the easiest of which are split passes to Casemiro and Vinícius Júnior. Playing into the forward would allow him to set to Casemiro, who could then either play Vinícius Júnior behind or, more realistically, switch play to Valverde high in the right-wing.

With these four patterns, it's clear that Kroos, Ramos, and Varane are the three key players in the build-up. As Real Madrid prepares to attack the opponents, it's these three players who pull the strings. As they circulate possession amongst themselves, they're looking for cracks in the opposition's system. Are they moving well horizontally? As they move, are their lines becoming stretched vertically? Are they overloading in one area? Have our players created a quantitative, qualitative, positional, or socio-affective superiority?

With their security in possession and their ability to hit intermediate and long-range targets, they offer Real Madrid a lot of security in the buildup, which allows them to focus their mental energy on constructing play.

Against high-pressing teams, it's common to see these patterns emerge, at least to break the first line or two and progress to midfield. Once Real Madrid gets to midfield, you'll often see the opponents settle into a more stable defensive structure.

When we speak of a team's formation, such as a 1-4-3-3 or a 1-4-4-2, what we're doing is addressing the team's standard defensive shape.

As teams settle into the middle block that formation is very clearly seen. That leads directly into the next part of Real Madrid's attacking tactics, setting up play to beat the middle block.

If you've read this chapter even remotely closely, you get one guess to figure out the three stars of the next chapter.

*Chapter 9*

# The Impact of Deep Distributions

One of the problems Zidane solved during the 2019/20 season was setting the point at which Real Madrid started their attack against the opposition's press. The previous season, one of the team's major issues was that their slow, indirect buildup allowed the opposition to comfortably transition into a very compact defensive shell. With little space to attack in the final third, Real Madrid was forced into the monotony of the U-shaped swing from one wing to the other.

The biggest issue is that beginning the attack on the opposition's lines in the final third means that vertical movements are more or less eliminated from the equation.

And that's not only vertical moves from the attacking team.

Granted, with players like Vinícius Júnior and Eden Hazard, giving them space to run at the defense puts them in a position where they can fully utilize their skill set to attack the opponent. As the attacking team moves higher into the final third the space disappears. Further, space between the lines is tougher to access.

And that's where we hit the point on the vertical movement of the defense. When you see a team drop all but one or two players behind the ball, sometimes all 11 within 30 yards of goal, the defense is attempting to set the match's initiative. Since they want to impose the initiative from defense, you could say it's a negative initiative they're imposing on the game.

However, a negative initiative is the right of the inferior team. You could also make the case that the winning team, attempting to see out the final minutes of the match, can also gain that negative initiative. By sitting back to protect the lead, they force the opposition into a proactive state. Since the opposition needs a goal or more to secure the result, the team in the lead can leverage the match state against the losing team.

When a team does look to initiate from the low block, the message they're sending to the attacking team is that they are going to reduce the playing area of the match, taking away access to the middle, and force the opponent to play through a wall of defenders.

When this happens, the lines become horizontally and vertically compact. The horizontal part is readily understood. By taking away the middle, you deny the most dangerous region of the field, preventing easy access to goal. That forces the team to funnel their attack into the wings, hampering the move to goal.

In terms of vertical compaction, teams are looking to deny space between the lines. As defensive teams park the bus and invite the opposition's attack into the final third of the field, you'll often see the defensive team keep anywhere from 5 to 10 yards between their lines. Regardless of how near the attackers are to each other, the defenders can then move from their disciplined position in the line to pressuring an opponent if there's a need.

*Drawing Opponents out of the Low Block*

Moving the low block is an incredibly difficult chore. Just ask Barcelona how they feel about it.

The reason teams move the ball from one wing to the other in that U-shaped motion is that they're trying to create space between the opposition's lines. By forcing the lines to slide left and right, attacking teams are praying that a gap emerges. The side-to-side motion is generally unproductive and a vertical element is necessary.

The other option, which Zidane and Real Madrid used to devastating effect, was to simply refuse to play the game upon the opposition's terms. Remember, that the team in the low block is trying to determine the game's initiative. They want a slow, predictable affair. The more indirect the opponent is in attack, the easier it is for the defending team to manage the flow of the game.

That's where Zidane used Kroos and the centerback so well. As the opposition set the low block, restricting the space for Real Madrid to attack, rather than ramming their head against the brick wall, Madrid set out to increase the space between the lines, primarily the vertical space.

Playing that negative pass to Kroos or Ramos allowed them to draw play back to the middle third, which forced the opposition to abandon the low block. Now, technically, I suppose one could argue the opponent could just sit in the low block and steadfastly refuse to play any higher, but that's a pretty rare sight and entirely against the spirit of the game.

*What's the Objective?*

This is where Real Madrid's attack looked to Zidane for a tactical solution. The solution wasn't necessarily a pattern of ball circulation. Instead, the solution was a pattern of opposition orientation.

If the game gets bogged down, playing backward allows Kroos and the centerbacks to quarterback play. With the whole pitch in their sightlines, they were scanning for visual cues signaling progression. If the opposition's lines were horizontally and vertically compact, the context of the game was telling them to just keep possession, just keep moving the ball in order to move the opposition's lines. As they circulated the ball along the back, occasionally playing the ball forward into the midfield or to the forwards, the deep-lying playmakers were looking for a specific visual cue. They were looking for the opposition to become unbalanced, overcommitting to one side of the field, which created gaps elsewhere.

Those forward passes into the midfield or forward lines were especially important. Even if the team used the first pass forward as a decoy, giving the appearance that they were now ready to attack the opposition, the reality is that the forward pass and subsequent negative forced the horizontal and vertical movement that Madrid needed. As the opposition collapsed on the receiving player, attempting to win the ball when it was played into the pressing structure, a negative pass out of the press created space for progression elsewhere.

So, for example, if Luka Modrić checked into the central channel, offering a positive pass to Sergio Ramos, Ramos might play the ball into Modrić in an attempt to pull the opposition's left-sided players closer to the center of the field. In turn, a player like Modrić senses when there's danger around him. Rather than taking additional touches or trying to turn, you'll see him play the ball back to someone like Ramos or Varane, which then allows for a pass to Carvajal in the wide-open spaces on the right. As Carvajal moves up the field, he can then look to create a 2v1 situation with his right-forward.

*Who are they targeting?*

Oftentimes, the exchange of short passes in the middle third was designed specifically with Kroos and Ramos in mind. As the team's preferred deep-lying playmakers, the left-sided partners looked to draw the opposition as close to that left side as possible.

Even if the objective was to target a player like Eden Hazard or Vinícius Júnior on the left, Kroos and Ramos could manipulate the opposition's lines with their switches of play and progressive passes.

If the team wanted to play to the left, making the opposition vertically compact in the middle third actually served them well. Hazard doesn't need much space to receive and Vinícius enjoys his runs behind the backline. So, drawing the opposition towards Ramos and Kroos created spatial conditions favoring the left-forwards.

By drawing the opposition close to Kroos and Ramos, Real Madrid was also creating the conditions for the long diagonal switch to the right.

That's really where you see the value of Kroos and Ramos in the attack. With their range and pinpoint accuracy, they had the ability to break the opposition's lines by simply playing over them.

And that's also where you see the intelligence of the two players. Not only are they press resistant, but they use their security and possession to confidently draw the opposition in, reducing the total area of defensive coverage. Once those visual cues are in place, both players show excellent awareness and timing when playing over the opposition's press.

Their passing percentages speak for themselves. It's not uncommon to see both players send over 60 passes in a game, often in the 90s for Kroos, while maintaining a mid-90s percent passing success rate.

Long diagonals can give the impression of a hit and hope approach, but it's the work that proceeds the long diagonal that creates the conditions for success.

By refusing to allow the opponent to set the initiative from defense, Real Madrid proactively circulates the ball in the middle third to keep the opposition from settling into a low block. In doing so, the long diagonals became a dangerous weapon.

Understanding the talent level of the wingers, we can see why Zidane wanted to create scenarios in which they were either 1v1, 2v1, or 2v2. Reducing the defensive coverage area of the opponent's middle block effectively created more space in the wings, which then increased the likelihood of success for the wingers.

*To the Drawing Board*

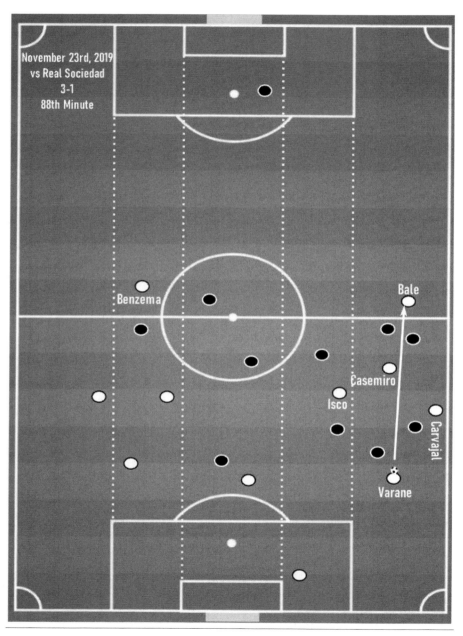

November 23rd, 2019
vs Real Sociedad
3-1
88th Minute

Benzema

Bale

Casemiro

Isco

Carvajal

Varane

Late in their win against Real Sociedad, we saw the impact of a deep distribution that broke La Real's lines. When Real Madrid circulated the ball along the back, Varane received the ball in the wing and was in a 4v3 situation with Carvajal, Isco, and Casemiro in support.

He also had Gareth Bale higher up the pitch, admittedly in a tight window.

As the Real Sociedad defenders pushed higher for the recovery, Varane gauged the positioning and momentum of the two deeper players. Though the passing lane to Bale was tight, Varane drove the ball on the ground into the path of Bale, splitting those two low defenders.

With Benzema drawing one defender out of position, moving him behind the bac line, Bale had space to receive behind the two defenders and take his first touch up the pitch.

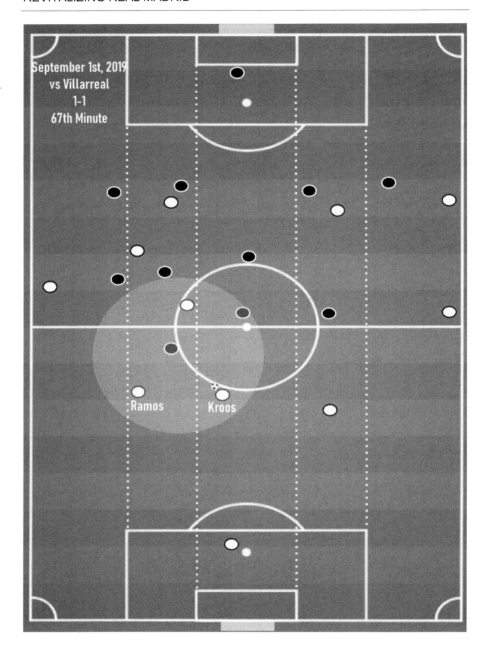

September 1st, 2019
vs Villarreal
1-1
67th Minute

Ramos

Kroos

Late in the game against Villarreal, we saw a direct example of that middle third point of engagement mentioned earlier. Kroos and Ramos orchestrated play from their role, trying to play from that circled area.

As you can see in the image, there is some space for progression on the left, using the wing to play around the opposition's defense.

However, space is also opening on the right for Carvajal. The switch to the right-wing is on and Carvajal has acres of space in front of him. He also has two teammates directly in front of him as well.

A good ball to Carvajal puts him in a position where he and the other two players can engage in a 3v2 against the left side of Villarreal's backline.

As Kroos and Ramos circulate the ball, one of the cues they are looking for is the opposition over-committing to one side of the pitch. In this example, Villarreal have six players committed higher up the park, defending in approximately three of the five vertical channels. The right midfielder is a few steps into the wing, but, on the whole, the line is fairly compact with the left midfielder approximately in the middle of the half space.

With the visual and sensory cues alerting the players to Villarreal's over-commitment, they sense the timing to attack the press.

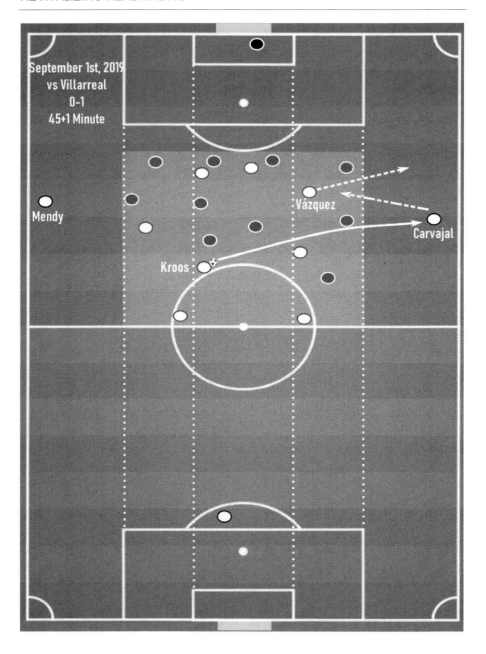

September 1st, 2019
vs Villarreal
0-1
45+1 Minute

Mendy

Vázquez

Carvajal

Kroos

Another way Real Madrid set up the long diagonal pass was through central overload.

During their away leg against Villarreal, Real Madrid used the outside-backs to offer width in the formation. The other eight Madrid field players lined up in the two half spaces and central channel.

As usual, Kroos, Ramos, and Varane were the three deepest players in the formation. Kroos had the ball in the central channel, very close to the left half space, as the side combined in the middle of the park. Those passes in the central layer area drew the Villareal defense in centrally.

With even the wide forwards pinching in, the Yellow Submarines were forced to respond even though they were already vertically compact, offering very little space between the lines. Situated in their low block, any forward pass from Real Madrid was typically met with a subsequent negative pass. Probing into the midfield served to make Villareal more compact, reducing the playing surface they were able to cover.

Once Villareal became too narrow, Kroos completed a switch of play to Carvajal in the right-wing. The outside-back decided to dribble into the left half space in an effort to pin the defense and create space for Vázquez in the wing. As Carvajal cut in, Vázquez swapped roles with him, becoming the width provider in the formation.

Rather than cutting the ball back out of the wings for Vázquez, Carvajal managed a tidy little combination with Luka Jović before setting up Gareth Bale's tying goal just before halftime.

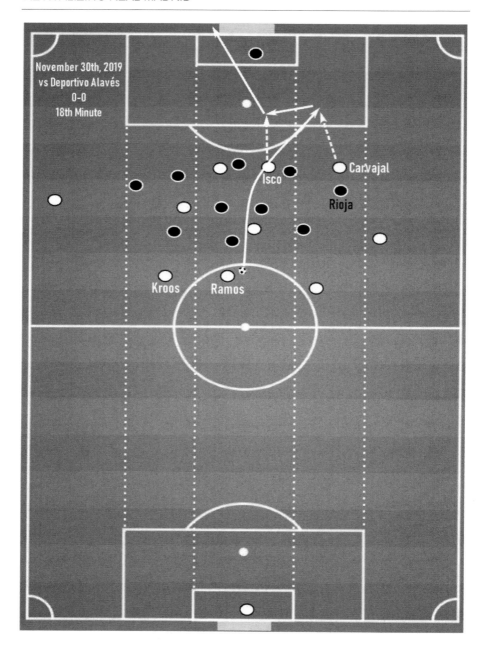

The final long distribution we'll cover comes to us from the November 30th matchup against Deportivo Alavés.

In theory, it's the simplest pass, a Route 1, point A to point B vertical ball. However, accurately executing this pass, especially against a low block, is incredibly difficult.

To set up the sequence, Bale and Isco were positioned in the central channel, pulling the centerbacks behind the rest of the backline.

Carvajal had initially made a run into the right half space that was not played, so Rioja seemed to forget about the right-back's presence. With the ball at Ramos's feet and plenty of time to pick out his pass, Carvajal gambled by staying in line with Bale and Isco in a nice little pocket of space in the right half space.

Signaling for the ball, Carvajal caught Ramos' attention. A gently lofted ball over the top met the end of Carvajal's run. He set the ball to Isco centrally, but the shot was pulled wide of the net.

It's also worth noting the role of Modrić. He essentially swapped rolls with Carvajal, taking on a deeper position in the wing. Though he's not actively engaged in the play, his starting point puts Rioja in a position where he releases Carvajal in preparation to press Modrić. Producing that little bit of indecision in Rioja allowed Carvajal to get behind the winger and get on the end of Ramos' chip uncontested.

To this point, Kroos has been one of the stars in the book. The way Zidane used him in the side's attacking tactics was pivotal to the title. So important, he deserves his own chapter.

*Chapter 10*

# The Kroos Role

One of the key elements of Real Madrid's performances, both in defense and attack, was the utilization of Toni Kroos. During the previous season, the German playmaker was largely deployed as a left-center attacking midfielder serving as one of the two players at the top of the midfield triangle.

That was one of the first things to change under Zidane. Rather than moving Kroos high up the pitch, he settled him into a deeper role. This role is very close to what we saw with Andrea Pirlo throughout his career. With Casemiro to his right performing the role of the midfield destroyer, Kroos was utilized as a regista. The regista, a deep-lying playmaker, is well-suited for a partnership with an aggressive ball-winner like the Brazilian.

Since Kroos and Casemiro fit the bill, Zidane set them out as part of a double pivot, with Kroos operating in the left half space. He was tasked with finding pockets of space outside of the opponent's press. In general, we saw Real Madrid use a central square at the back. Ramos and Varane were the base of the square, while Kroos and Casemiro operated higher up the pitch. Within that square, Kroos and Ramos were situated on the left-hand side. Between the two players, they worked to orchestrate the attack and manipulate the opponent's press to free each other to act as a deep distributor.

*The Half Space Hotspot*

In Kroos' role in particular, especially during the buildup, when Real Madrid faced a middle block, he frequently took his position just outside the press in the left half space. Starting outside of the opponent's press created a pocket to not only receive, but also take a positive first touch and release passes to long targets. Rather than painstakingly playing through the opponent, Real Madrid used Kroos' range and pinpoint accuracy to play over them with a long diagonal ball.

As a right-footed player, he was equally capable of making an across body pass to the left-wing and half spaces. From his role, Real Madrid had access to every part of the pitch.

That was one of the strengths of this Real Madrid side. As opposition defenses were naturally vertically and horizontally compact, Real Madrid's reliance on Kroos to play over the defense to the right or through the defense to the left and middle gave them a variety of options in attack. Between Kroos and Ramos, entry into the final third was almost a given.

As the team progressed into the final third of the pitch, we frequently saw Kroos start a little deeper than he had the previous season. Rather than moving to the top of the box, he typically started a little bit deeper, allowed the opposition to drop fully into a low block, and then identified pockets of space outside of the block that would allow him to pull the strings from outside their press.

With the left-sided forward typically being a dribble first player, Kroos' orientation in the left half space gave his left-forward the isolation he preferred. When it wasn't the left-forward moving into that pocket of space, it was the left-back. Regardless of whether it was Mendy or Marcelo, Kroos tended to favor receiving a negative pass, drawing the defense towards him, and then playing his defensive partner behind the opposition lines. Whether it was a left-forward or a left-back, Kroos used his starting point as a means of manipulating the opponent's pressing structure, creating pockets of space for his teammates to attack, be it on the dribble or on the receiving end of a pass.

*Protecting the Left Half Space*

In terms of his defensive contributions, this is really where Zidane's tactics were spot on. Having seen the joy opponents had experienced attacking Real Madrid's left side during the two previous seasons as both Kroos and Marcelo struggled to get back defensively, Zidane figured out how to release the left-back, allowing him to operate primarily as an attacking winger, while also denying the opposition the opportunity to counterattack behind him.

Sitting a little bit deeper, Real Madrid always had a body to deny those passes into space. It was far more difficult for them to draw Ramos into the midfield to pressure the ball. The presence of Kroos in that left half space gave his captain the ability to stay at home, limiting the distance he had to cover when tracking into midfield.

That was a game-changer for this Real Madrid team.

Opponents could no longer counterattack Real Madrid's left, and, if they wanted to counterattack at all, they were going to run into either Kroos or Casemiro.

The added benefit of Kroos' new starting point was that it limited the space both Ramos and Casemiro had to cover in defensive transitions. Even though

Casemiro has been a world-class defensive midfielder for many years now, it's unrealistic to ask a single player to cover the full width of the pitch, regardless of how well he reads the game.

With Kroos' deeper position, Casemiro was able to focus his attention on the central and right-sided regions of the pitch. The result was another fantastic season, possibly his best, safeguarding Real Madrid in transition. In turn, he created freer conditions for the players in front of him.

*Kroos' Last Four Seasons by the Numbers*

To better understand Kroos' performance over the past four years, The following radars offer a visual where, unlike the forwards' radar, the endpoints of the Kroos radars are the four-year bests from the man himself. Whatever his statistical highs were the past four seasons, those measures set the endpoints of the radars.

If you've tracked his career closely, you certainly won't be surprised by the level of consistency in many of the categories. When looking at his total and successful actions, long passes plus the completion percentage, pass totals and success rate, and passes to the final third, there really is very little variation.

However, each season presented a new set of demands from the German. In each radar, there are typically one or two gaps in performance.

# Toni Kroos
## 2016/17

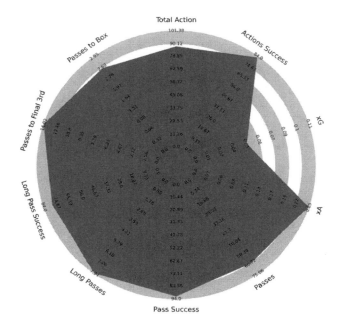

For example, during the 2016/17 season, Kroos gapped significantly in xG, with minor gaps in passes to the box in total actions.

Elsewhere on the board his numbers either set the standard or are very close to it. One of the clear standouts from all four radars is his efficiency. When you look at his success rates, his pass completion percentage is always in the low 90s and his long pass success is right around 80%, both marks well ahead of the positional average, especially his long pass percentage.

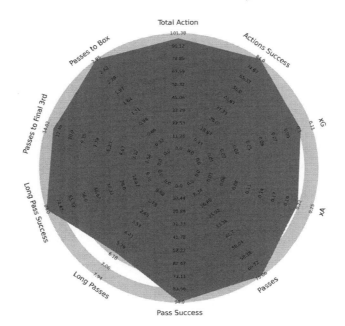

# Toni Kroos
## 2017/18

Moving along to 2017/18, passes to the box reached a four-year high with total actions nearing the high mark.

He made a nice recovery in the xG category, showing a greater threat to goal, plus he posted nice xA (expected assists per 90 minutes) stats.

The one gap in the radar is in the long passes P90 minutes category. Compared to the four-year high of 7.94, Kroos averaged just 5.86 long passes per game in Ronaldo's final season. He was accurate in 84% of those passes, which is higher than an average player's total passing percentage, which is a really incredible feat.

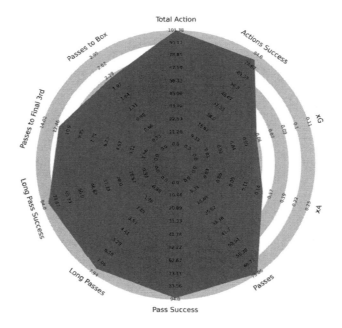

Moving on to Zidane's gap year, Kroos was as involved as ever in the team's play, setting the 4-year standard of 75.06 passes per 90 minutes. He played nearly as many long passes per game as he did during the 2016/17 season, which represents the 4-year high, but his long pass accuracy dropped to 80%.

Even though Kroos was more involved in the team's overall play, there are still two gaps in the radar.

The first surrounds xG and xA. With Real Madrid playing a 1-4-3-3 during the 2018/19 season and Kroos occupying the left-center mid role, he played higher up the pitch than he did in 2019/20. Madrid went point down in the midfield, meaning there were two attacking mids. In a more advanced area, it would be reasonable to assume that Kroos' xG and xA stats would be higher in 2018/19 as opposed to other seasons.

The same goes for passes to the final third and passes to the box. Positioned higher up the pitch, his marks really should either set the standard or be close to it.

This radar could very easily represent the whole team's season. With a 0.53 (24%) decline in xG, the entire team struggled to create meaningful chances to goal.

# Toni Kroos
## 2019/20

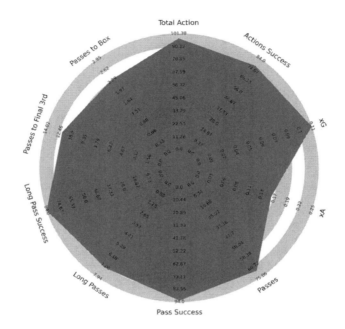

Finally, looking at 2019/20, the year Kroos dropped into a deeper, regista midfield role, his xA, passes to the box, and passes to the final third continued to lag behind.

However, his passing efficiency was as good as ever. Plus, he was highly engaged, nearing the radar endpoint in total actions.

The fact that there's a slight improvement from the previous season's radar, all while playing a deeper role in the midfield, shows the impressive work Kroos put into the season.

*To the Drawing Board*

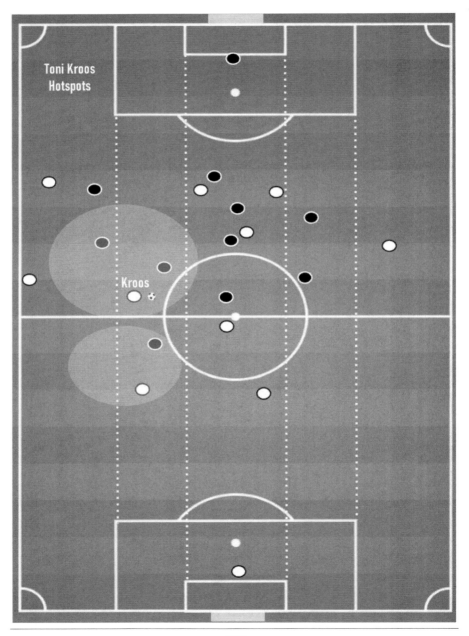

One of the beauties of Toni Kroos' game is the simplicity of it. He's not the flashy playmaking #10, nor is he the dynamic dribbling #8. His strength is in his vision and distribution.

As you watch Kroos play, you almost get the sense that you're watching a reincarnation of vintage Pirlo or Xabi Alonso, though perhaps without Xabi's defensive bite. Much like his regista predecessors, Kroos operates best outside of the opposition's press. From outside of the opponent's defensive shape, he can then pick up his head and identify the vulnerabilities in their structure.

There are two spots on the field where Kroos is most likely to receive the ball. Both are in the left half space, one is in his defensive half of the field, the other in the attacking half.

Those locations fit specific functions. Once Real Madrid has progressed into the middle third of the pitch you'll see Kroos transition from a more fluid role that is designed to help the team break out of the defensive third, to a more concrete location higher up the pitch. As opponents settle into their middle block, Kroos takes up his spot in the left half space, just outside of their defensive shape. From that point, he can utilize his range to hit the full width of the pitch.

As a right-footed player playing on the left side of the field, touching the ball to his right-hand side allows him to drive the ball the full width of the pitch, opening up the possibility of playing into his right-forward. If he prefers to play into a left-sided or central teammate, he can use his body orientation to sell the long diagonal to the right while, in fact, setting up for the crossbody strike to his left or center.

As Real Madrid breaks into the attacking third of the pitch, he's very disciplined in offering that deep outlet outside of the opposition's low block. Once he receives the ball in that second circle, high up the half space, he can either set up his left-forward or outside-back for a cross into the box, swing the ball across the pitch to switch the point of attack, or take action himself, either through a cross or shot.

Remaining outside of the opponent's pressing structure gives him more time and space to orchestrate play. Once Madrid enter the attacking third of the field, opponents are quick to follow, becoming horizontally and vertically compact, especially prioritizing the middle of the pitch. If Real Madrid is going to play, opponents want them funneling the ball into the wings. At least at that point, opponents can simplify their defensive work by reducing the number of variables they have to defend against.

With a low block intact, Kroos' role becomes incredibly important. As mentioned earlier, his presence in that left half space serves to protect Ramos if the opponent wins the ball and starts a counterattack. On the attacking side of Zidane's tactics, the deep outlet to Kroos gives Real Madrid both a deep playmaker and a press resistant player when they're under pressure.

Looking at Kroos' pass map against Atlético Madrid, one of the things that immediately stands out is the range on some of these passes. With his half space positioning, the shorter to intermediate-range passes in the left-wing, left half space, and central channel are fairly routine. For those longer-range passes, sending the ball from the half space reduces the flight time of the ball as compared to distributions from the wing. The benefit of half space service rather than the central channel is that it also pulls opponents closer to one side of the pitch, bringing up additional space in the far wing for the right-forward and outside-back.

Even with his impeccable long-range deliveries, Kroos does manage to diversify his approach, keeping opponents off balance. Depending on who's playing left-forward, Kroos has a number of options to play on the left-hand side of the pitch. Add in the fact that Benzema frequently drops into the left half space and there's a very strong trio of players available to Kroos on the left.

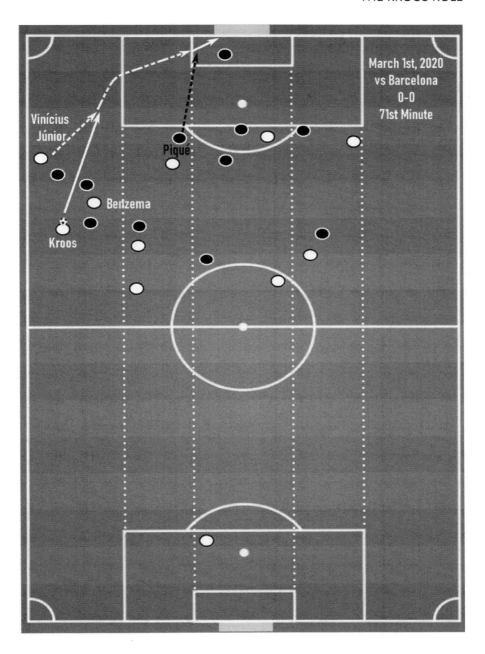

Vinícius Júnior

Pique

Benzema

Kroos

March 1st, 2020
vs Barcelona
0-0
71st Minute

The home leg of El Clasico proved just how dangerous Kroos can be when playing to the left side of the pitch. Engaged in a 3v3 against Barcelona, Kroos, Benzema, and Vinícius Júnior held the ball high in the left-wing. With Kroos on the ball, Benz made his classic checking run into the half space, pulling Nélson Semedo with him. That opened up a major gap behind the three Barcelona defenders.

Martin Braithwaite was the player nearest Vinícius Júnior. With a forward dropping deep to help out defensively, Kroos saw an opportunity to strike.

As you watch the play, you see Kroos raise his arm and signal where he wants Vinícius Júnior to run. The veteran midfielder saw the passing lane early on, well before the young Brazilian. Once Vinícius Júnior saw what Kroos was directing him to do, he made a darting run behind Braithwaite, latching on to a perfectly weighted through ball from Kroos.

Vinícius Júnior then cut inside on his right foot, dribbled close to the corner of the 6-yard box, and smashed a shot off of Gerard Piqués' leg into the goal, giving Real Madrid the game-winner and a clear path to the La Liga crown.

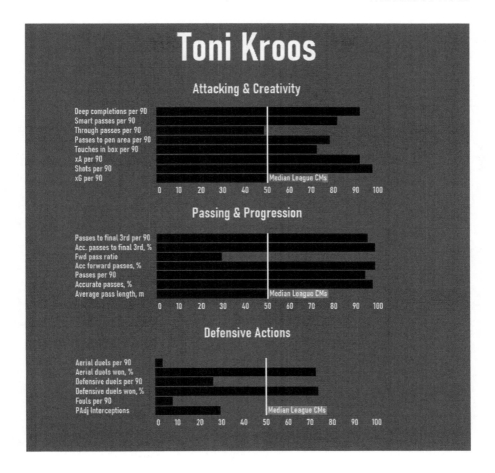

To contextualize Toni Kroos' performance in 2019/20, the player profile rates his statistical contributions against La Liga's other central midfielders.

In terms of his passing marks, he rates in the 90th percentile or higher almost across the board. In the passing in progression portion of the chart, Kroos is either the best in the league or among the top few players in nearly every category. Three of those categories measure passing efficiency, an area where Kroos has no equal.

The only two categories on the wrong side of the league median line are through passes per 90 and forward pass ratio.

But even those are easily understood. Since the stats are measured against all La Liga center midfielders, a deep-lying player like Kroos will have fewer opportunities for through passes than a box-to-box or attacking midfielder. Plus, given his role in the build-up, the forward pass ratio is neither surprising nor troublesome.

Remember that within the build-up, the objective is not simply to play forward. The objective is to set conditions for a successful attack. For an indirect, possession-based team like Real Madrid, that often requires negative passes to move the defense. By moving the defense, the team in possession is doing the prep work. They move the ball to move the defense, creating superiorities higher up the pitch. Once those superiorities are in place and become accessible, that's the time to attack. Until then, deep-lying players like Kroos must patiently move the ball in an attempt to provoke the setup.

Finally, looking at the defensive actions section, his marks are still relatively low almost across the board. He doesn't engage in many aerial or defensive duels, but, when he does, he's generally very successful.

Playing deeper in Zidane's formation, it's reasonable to expect better numbers in the defensive categories, especially possession adjusted interceptions (PAdj Interceptions) which puts a player's total interceptions per game in ratio to the team's possession percentage. Players in possession-dominant teams tend to record fewer interceptions per game simply because there are so few opportunities. So, leveling the playing field with possession adjusted interceptions, we can objectively say that Kroos' 30th percentile rank is low for the position.

But Kroos isn't in there for his defensive work. If anything, from a defensive standpoint, his greatest contribution is simply positioning himself in the left half space while still producing incredible attacking numbers. Fixing his starting point became more of a preventative measure. Rather than Kroos taking on Casemiro-like defensive responsibilities on the left side of the pitch, his presence alone solved the problem of allowing teams to counterattack into the left half space. With Kroos, the threat vanished.

And that's where credit is due to Zidane.

Systematizing the midfield to solve the tactical issues of the previous season was a stroke of brilliance. With clear and defined roles, as well as greater discipline in the team's rest defense, Zidane's midfield safeguarded the backline while also solving issues within the team's attacking tactics.

# Chapter 11

# Systematizing the Midfield

Dropping Toni Kroos deeper in the midfield was certainly Zidane's biggest tactical tweak in that area of the pitch. Pairing him in a double pivot with Casemiro, the two contributed to one of Europe's best defenses and offering attacking freedom to their teammates.

With an in-depth analysis of the Kroos role in the books, it's time to move on to the other three midfielders.

*Casemiro: The Destroyer*

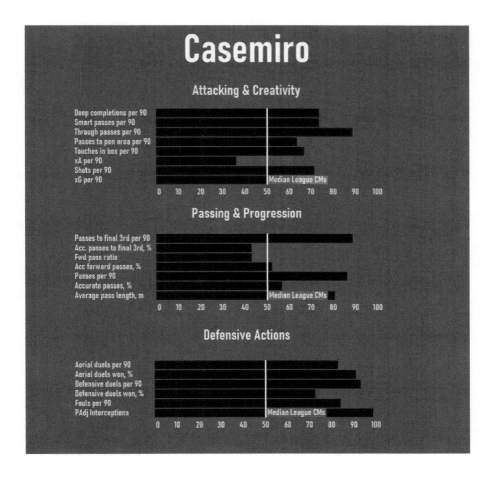

When assessing Casemiro, the first place you have to look is his defensive work. After all, that is his role within the team. He's the midfield destroyer. With an expertise in ending the opponent's attack, his primary role on the pitch is to safeguard the backline and cut out danger before opponents can really break into a full-fledged attack.

His player profile compares him statistically to La Liga's center midfielders. Casemiro's worst statistical category is in the defensive duels won percentage stat where he rates in the 70th percentile. His aerial duels won, defensive duels per 90 minutes, and possession adjusted interceptions all rate in the 90th percentile or better.

In terms of his attacking contribution, Casemiro is widely regarded as a weak spot in the buildup. He does have the occasional bad giveaway, but it is important to remember that if you're the weak spot when compared to Kroos, Ramos, and Varane, there's certainly the danger of skewing the assessment.

His attacking creativity profile rates very well, but it's his passing in progression that's more significant. As the team's number six, the major positives are his involvement, which is categorized by his passes per 90, as well as his passes to the final third per 90 minutes. In terms of his passing efficiency, there's definitely room for improvement, but for a ball-winning defensive midfielder to rate right around the league median in passing efficiency, there's not too much room for complaint.

Still, he is to Kroos what Gennaro Gattuso was to Andrea Pirlo. One is the dominant defensive presence in the midfield, an absolute warrior in defensive duels, the other is the majestic, deep-lying playmaker.

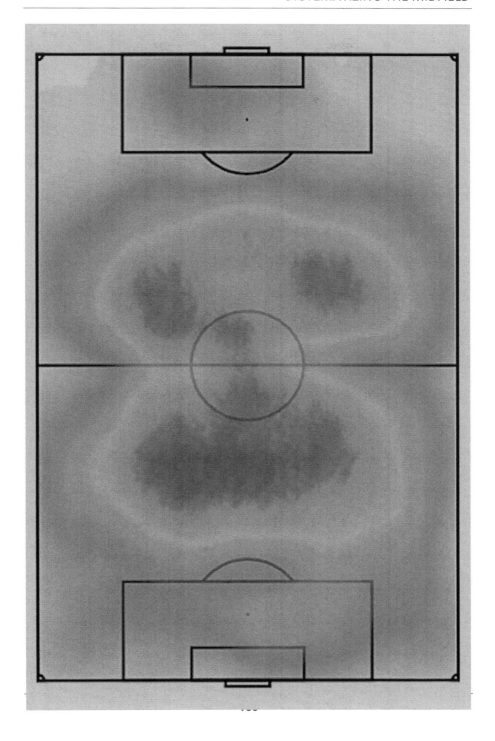

Studying Casemiro's heat map shows just how much ground he covered in the midfield. Right about at that point where his team is entering the defensive third, Casemiro's heat map lights up. The hottest points on the map, he absolutely owns the area just in front of his centerbacks. While he'll slide into the wings if necessary, his preference is to safeguard the central channel and half spaces. Just beyond that bright central area, there's another hue showing he'll cover the full width of the box.

His heat map has an hourglass figure, becoming narrow near midfield. It lights up again in the central parts of the midfield circle, then again in the left and right half spaces in the attacking half of the field.

What the heat maps are doing is tracking where a player takes his touches. In Casemiro's case, there are definitely his attacking contributions to take into consideration. He does help with the build-out and offers a deep outlet once the team is engaged in the attacking half of the field.

That said, these areas also correspond to where he's most active defensively. Remember that tackles and interceptions factor in his first touches. Whether he's protecting the backline and his defensive half, counterpressing in the attacking half, or intercepting a pass due to an effective man-marking high-press, Casemiro shines brightest in his defensive contributions.

*To the Drawing Board*

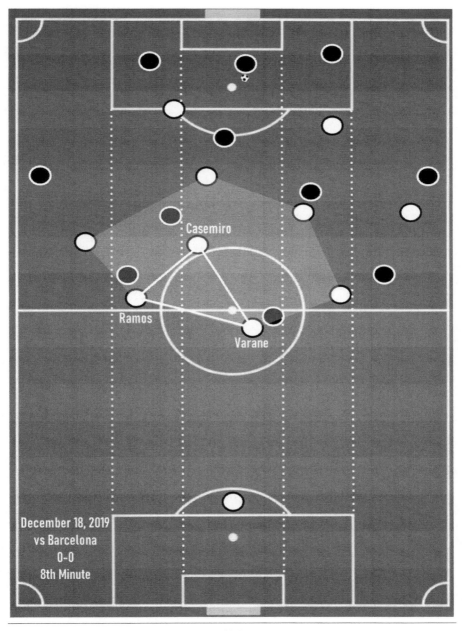

Speaking of the man-marking high-press, Casemiro deserves the spotlight for his role in this particular defensive tactic.

The players ahead of him certainly deserve credit. After all, it is their quick counterpressing, ability to force negative passes, and discipline to man-mark that forces the opposition into those vulnerable, long-range passes.

Once those long-range passes are played, it's incredible how often Casemiro's the one on the end of the pass.

It all starts with his positioning. While his midfield partners enjoy some freedom in the man-marking high-press, which occasionally requires them to follow their marks into Real Madrid's attacking third of the pitch, Casemiro usually stays well connected to his backline. Knowing that the opposition only has a few options, usually the long diagonal ball into the wings or the long pass into the center forward with the hope of winning the second ball, Casemiro sits in the gap between his backline and midfield partners. From that gap, he's not only man-marking, but he's looking for long-range deliveries to intercept.

In the first Clásico of the season, Real Madrid was engaged in the man-marking high-press. The only player left unmarked was the right-back, Nélson Semedo. Even then, Ferland Mendy was close enough to contest any pass to Semedo.

Within the man-marking high-press, the midfielders' roles were well defined by Zinedine Zidane. Kroos and the right-center midfielder were given explicit instructions to find a mark and stick with him. Casemiro, while also man-marking a more centrally located opponent, had to find the balance between man-marking and protecting the backline. Finding that balance is one of his greatest strengths as a player anyway, so, in handing him that role, Zidane was putting him in a position for success. Prioritizing Casemiro's ball-winning talents in the defensive tactics gave the players in front of him so much freedom and security in the attack. Knowing that Casemiro had their back and was ready to reclaim possession gave the attackers the assurance that they could be brave in possession, that they could try the spectacular without hurting the team.

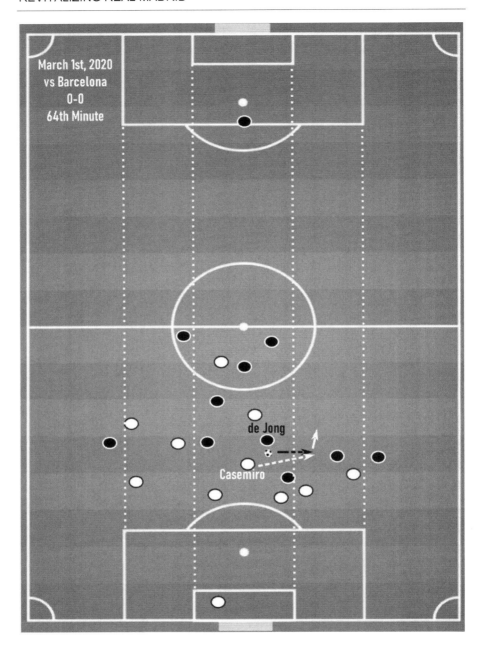

When opponents did manage to break through the man-marking high-press, Casemiro's connectivity with the centerbacks is incredibly reliable. When he was engaged as the pressure defender, Ramos and Varane were afforded coverage, which allowed them to remain in deeper positions.

When El Clásico made its way to Madrid, there was a sequence in the 64th minute that saw Frenkie de Jong in possession of the ball entering the final third. Antoine Griezmann was in front of him and Messi to his right. Real recovered well defensively, leaving de Jong with limited options.

Rather than forcing a bad pass to a tightly marked teammate, de Jong tried to initiate play through the dribble.

The issue is that Casemiro was able to block off the path to the middle, funneling de Jong out wide. As the Dutchman entered the left half space, Casemiro closed down the space between the two. The Brazilian put in a strong tackle, taking the ball off of de Jong.

One of the points to emphasize is how perfectly positioned Casemiro was from the start of the sequence. Forming a right triangle with Ramos and Varane, Casemiro held the high point. His positioning, as well as de Jong's awareness of Casemiro's defensive clout, funneled the Dutchman away from the central channel.

Earlier in the book, we looked at how teams can impose initiative on the match through their defensive tactics.

On an individual basis, that's exactly what Casemiro does. Whether he's engaged in a 1v1 duel, funneling play away from dangerous areas, or using his hyper-developed senses of awareness and anticipation to intercept passes,

Casemiro's the type of player who can impose his will on the game purely from a defensive standpoint. Given all the white-collar playmakers on the team, his blue-collar mentality may very well make him the most important player on the team.

*Luka Modrić: The Magician*

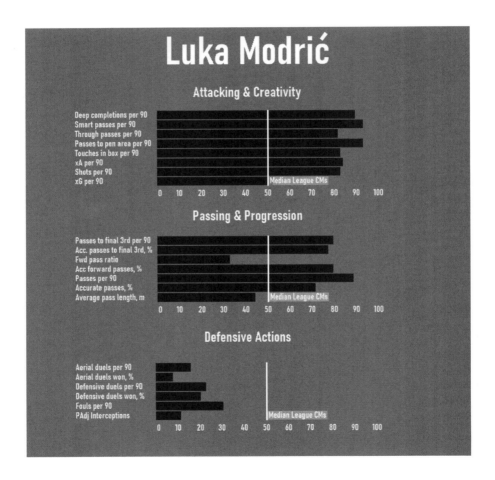

As the right-center midfielder, Luka Modrić enjoys an attack-first role in the team's tactics. While he still contributes to the defensive side of the game with his counterpressing, his player profile clearly shows defensive actions are not a strength. But, again, counterpressing and contributing to the man-marking high-press doesn't always show up on the stat sheet. In those regards, Modrić has proven himself an effective defender.

Where he really shines is in the attacking and creativity categories.

With the exception of xG per 90, which ranks just ahead of the league median for center midfielders, the 2018 Ballon d'Or winner earns 80th percentile marks or better. In terms of passes to the penalty area and deep completions, which are non-crossing passes that are targeted within 20 meters of an opponent's goal, and smart passes, which are creative ways of breaking pressure, there are a few in the league that best Modrić.

His passing and progression stats show a similar story. Like Kroos, his forward pass ratio lags behind as does his average pass length. Those numbers are completely acceptable given this team's style of play and his role within the attacking tactics.

What really stands out in this section of the profile is the combination of high usage and high efficiency in all passing categories. He simply hasn't shown any signs of slowing down. Especially now that Federico Valverde can offer rotation at right-center mid, Modrić looked as fit and energetic at the end of the season as he did at the start.

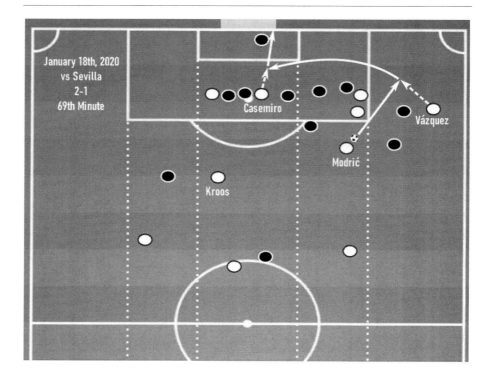

His fitness levels were a critical part of the team's success. Given the number of teams Real Madrid faces that set up in a low block, if Real Madrid is unable to pull them higher up the pitch, it's Modrić's work in the right half space that offers creative solutions for breaking the press.

Now, Sevilla is not typically a side that will settle into a low block. They prefer to engage in a high-press, winning the ball higher up the pitch to increase the ease of their attacking sequences. However, during the 69th minute of their match in January, Sevilla dropped all but one player into the defensive third of the field.

Positioned in the right half space, just outside of the box, Modrić's responsibility was to find a pocket of space just outside of the press. From that pocket of space, his teammates could play into him and allow him to use his vision and creativity to play a ball that beat the press.

In this instance, he received the ball, drew in the opposition's defense, and played a simple ball onto the run of Vázquez. The right-forward whipped a brilliant ball into the box, finding the head of Casemiro for the winning goal.

It's a simple action in this case, but, with so little time and space in the attacking third, it's a role that so many players get wrong. Strained by the pressure of nearby opponents, it's common to see players shut off mentally and succumb to the overwhelming nature of the moment.

Even in the attacking third of the pitch, it's very rare to see Modrić feel pressured by the bodies around him. His calm, composed mindset allows him to cut through the noise and chaos in the match. He's a player who seems like he's always in control of the situation. Better yet, he's always in control of himself, approaching the game with clarity of mind.

*Federico Valverde: The Swiss Army Knife*

Coming into the 2019/20 season, there was an assumption that Valverde would offer rotation options for Casemiro, Kroos, and Modrić. The young Uruguayan had a solid, though not spectacular, season in 2018/19, so the expectation was that he could continue growing into a midfield role with Real Madrid. Though he got his start as a defensive midfielder, his versatility throughout the pitch was one of the aspects that appealed to Zinedine Zidane. Not only did he have the opportunity to give Casemiro the occasional day of rest, but he offered a tantalizing skill set that Zidane could use either in a double pivot or as a more attack-oriented midfielder on the right.

Though he did get the occasional game at defensive mid or on the left in that Kroos role, where we saw him most often was as the more attack-oriented right-sided midfielder. There are a few reasons for this.

First, in the defensive and defensive transition phases of the game, he offered excellent counterpressing, sound tackling technique, and a strong presence in the midfield. Those defensive midfielder roots came in handy, especially in the counterpress. With Real Madrid among La Liga's best in possession, finishing second to Barcelona with 57.91%, much of their possession came in the opposition's half of the pitch. Upon losing the ball, Valverde's defensive instincts immediately caught the eye.

Rather than making a hopeful run up the pitch, assuming that low percentage plays would reach their completion, Valverde showcased a more circumspect approach. His eye for detail allowed him to quickly assess the opposition's chances of success, enabling him to make early adjustments. That recognition and early action, combined with his extraordinary ability to quickly cover ground, made him a menace as the opposition tried to play out of Real Madrid's counterpress.

Even if his objective wasn't to win the ball, he was exceptional in denying forward passing opportunities. Since many opponents looked to counterattack against Real Madrid, his ability to force the first or second pass backward was a tremendous quality for this side. In buying those extra seconds, he bought time for his midfield and outside-back teammates to get back into their defensive shape, ensuring the opposition would have to play through a press rather than maraud through open space.

In terms of his attacking contribution, we have to make a two-fold distinction. Valverde's role as the right-center midfielder was typically dependent upon his right-forward partner. If Rodrygo, Bale, or Vázquez filled that role, we saw Valverde more frequently utilized as a support midfielder.

Since those three are proficient both on the dribble and running in behind the defense, they like to take up higher positions on the pitch, either isolating themselves with a 1v1 with a defender or putting themselves in a position where they can run off of Benzema's movement, getting behind the backline into goal.

If the right-forward fit more of a midfield mold, the interchange on the right was incredibly fluid. For instance, if it was Isco operating on the right-hand side of the pitch, you'd frequently see the Spaniard drifting not only into the right half space but more or less in a free role moving across the top line. He was more of a roaming playmaker than a right-forward. With Isco roaming across the pitch, that opened up the wing for Carvajal and Valverde. If Real Madrid was coming from a scenario that forced them to defend in their defensive half of the field, it was typically Carvajal who played more conservatively, allowing Valverde to make darting runs into the right-wing.

That's where the Uruguayan was so dangerous.

I've already mentioned his exceptional pace. When the team transitioned from defending deep in their own half to hitting the opposition on the break, Valverde's ability to get behind the opposition's left-back added a whole new dimension to Real Madrid.

In some sense, you could argue his movement in the wings was reminiscent of a younger Cristiano Ronaldo and Gareth Bale, very direct and explosive in his wing progression. While not nearly as technically skilled as the other two, his blistering pace reduced the need for exceptional dribbling qualities.

When Real Madrid looked to spring the counterattack, especially when Vinícius Júnior was on the bench, Valverde was an outlet they looked to frequently. He became one of the most important transition attacking pieces on the team. You could argue that his influence in transition was only superseded by Vinícius himself.

The second aspect of his attacking contribution was in open possessions. As the team looked to build out in their defensive half, Valverde took a higher role, allowing Kroos and Casemiro to orchestrate the build-out.

With Valverde higher up the pitch, he was able to connect with his right-forward, giving Real Madrid the high and wide overload on the right, a preferred tactic for Zinedine Zidane.

As a side progressed into the attacking half of the pitch, Valverde transitioned into more of a traditional midfield role. If the ball was on the left-hand side of the pitch he'd pinch inside to offer coverage and give a central presence. He also gave them another aerial target in the box, a threat that only Benzema and Bale (when he played) offered among the highest positioned players.

As a ball moved to the right-hand side of the pitch, Valverde typically interacted with his right-forward and Carvajal to create crossing opportunities. Since Valverde could interchange with either of those two players, attacking third interactions on the right-hand side of the pitch were a position of strength for Real Madrid.

Valverde himself could either take up a high and wide position in preparation for sending a cross or start in the half space to offer combination opportunities to his teammates. That, in turn, allowed them to send their crosses or passes from the half spaces rather than the wings, a much higher percentage play. If need be, the young Uruguayan could also drop deeper into the wing allowing Carvajal to make a diagonal run from the wing into the half space, more or less in a straight line from his starting point to the center of the goal.

Valverde's tactical adaptability and Swiss army knife functionality were foundational to Real Madrid's right-sided attacking tactics.

He and Modrić have two very different skill sets, the Croatian offering greater technical execution and vision, whereas the Uruguayan offers a greater presence in the counterattack and counterpress.

Beyond those distinctions, Valverde's assimilation into the right-sided attacking midfield role created conditions that allowed his teammates to find success. Whether it was just the assurance that Valverde was present and ready to counterpress if they lost the ball or his ability to take on any of his teammates' responsibilities on that right-hand side of the pitch, his ability to adapt his contribution to the team's needs allowed his teammates to play a more dynamic, lively attacking style.

While there's certainly still room for growth, especially in terms of his passing range and vision, the 2019/20 season was a massive step forward for Valverde. As Luka Modrić continues to march towards his Real Madrid exit, it's Valverde who is now the natural successor to that right-sided midfield role.

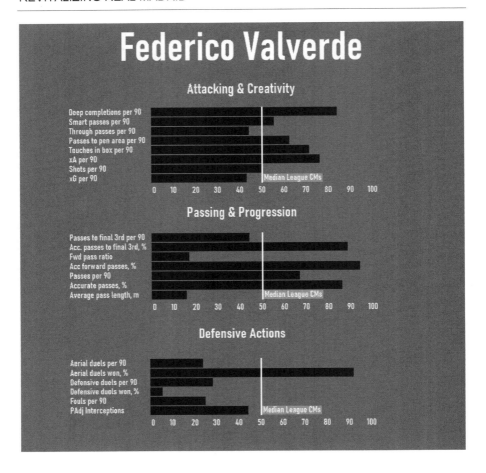

Not quite the passer that Modrić is, Valverde's perhaps better known for his defensive contributions. With that in mind, if you looked at his defensive actions profile with a state of shock and disbelief, remember that this is a Real Madrid team that's very good at funneling play into particular regions of the pitch. The right-sided central midfielder was an attack first position within the team's tactics, so the defensive responsibilities were mostly limited to counterpressing and participating in the man-marking high-press.

Progressed into the defensive half. Both showed that they were committed to the cause, dropping in to help out with the press.

Even though Valverde needs to continue improving his understanding of the game and passing precision, his attacking statistics profile really well.

He was among the best center midfielders in La Liga in his forward pass accuracy percentage, accuracy of passes to the final third, and total pass accuracy. It was an efficient performance from the young Uruguayan. Volume can certainly pick up, but even there, nearly the 70th percentile for passes per 90 minutes it's nothing to gawk at.

In the attacking and creativity section, you can see his influence in the attacking third. His deep completions per 90 minutes gives a sign of his presence high up the pitch and his involvement as the team begins the move to goal. Those deep completions are coupled with his high percentage of touches in the box, xA per 90, and passes to the penalty area.

Valverde and Modrić played vital roles in Real Madrid's attack. High on the right, their connection with the right-forward was a big part of the team's approach.

*Chapter 12*

# Attacking Pairs

With all the adjustments in defensive tactics, there was still work to be done on the other side of the ball. Without Ronaldo in the lineup for the first time in a decade, the club experienced a massive regression, dropping their goals per game average from 2.47 to 1.66. There was a clear reduction in the expected calculations as well. Moving from 2.23 during the 2017/18 season all the way down to 1.70 in 2018/19, a 24% reduction.

Despite more possession with the Lopetegui coached team and more effective counterattacks with Solari, the club suffered from Ronaldo's absence in the lineup. Hazard was supposed to be the cure, contributing to the team as both a goal scorer and a playmaker, but his first season in Madrid was a forgettable one. When he did play, he was generally very good, especially in his link-up with Benzema. Most of the club's highest xG outputs came during Hazard's starts.

But as the saying goes, the best ability is availability. Sadly, the Belgian was never able to find his rhythm. In and out of the lineup, fitness and injuries plagued his season.

Analyzing the games he did manage to play, the biggest positive was definitely the way he and Benzema gelled almost instantly. The two looked like they had been playing together for years. Hazard, a versatile player who is capable of receiving out wide, dropping between the lines, or switching with the center forward, seemed like the perfect fit for Benzema. With the Frenchman preferring to drift away from the central channel into the left half space, attempting to pull the right-centerback into midfield with him, he and Hazard seemed to have a great understanding of each other with one pulling and the other responding to the run.

*Left-Sided Pairings*

That left-sided pairing encapsulates exactly what Zidane hoped to achieve higher up the pitch. In order to generate superiorities, Zidane's attacking tactics looked to create attacking pairs on either wing. With Benzema frequently dropping into the left half space it's natural that his partner was the left-forward.

If Hazard or Isco received the start on the left, the interaction between the left-forward and Benzema was rather fluid. With all of those three players capable of playing in the wings, half space, and central channel, it was merely a matter of pulling the defense out of their shape and moving off of each other. If Benzema dropped into midfield, Isco or Hazard would then slide centrally. If the left-forward remained in the wing, you might see Benzema stay a little higher in the half space or look to drop as a support option.

If Vinícius Júnior got the start at left-forward the relationship adapted to the Brazilian's skill set. A player who loves a 1v1 duel and is electric in open space, Benzema would still drop into the left half space, but the objective was to unleash Vinícius Júnior pace and direct dribbling style. That's where the left-forward partnership was tailored to the youngster.

As Benz dropped into the left half space, the objective was to pull the right-centerback into midfield with him. If he could accomplish that, the opposition's right-back was left without defensive coverage. Benzema didn't even necessarily need the ball at his feet, he simply needed to make the movement to attract the centerback.

Vini Jr's dribbling efficiency could certainly use some improvement. He averaged 8.86 attempts per 90, which was 4th most in La Liga, behind only Adnan Januzaj, Lionel Messi, and Ousmane Dembélé. However, his 47% dribbling success rate was among the worst at the position.

He is still a young player who has a tendency to put his head down and just run at his opponent. The next two years will be vital in his development. One of the necessities will be identifying when the dribble is on and when to prioritize playing off of teammates. There is certainly a sense that, at the moment, when he receives the ball he's too eager to achieve something spectacular. Flair and dynamism are great, but at times it does get in the way of the team's tactics. Cheap losses by forcing the dribble in bad spots made the team quickly transition away from structured attacks, making the players expend energy in the counterpress.

That said, when he's on his game, you won't find a more dynamic player in this Real Madrid side. If he can continue developing his relationship with Benzema, improving his understanding of how to play off of a forward who likes to drop into midfield, and improve his dribbling efficiency as well, the sky's the limit.

*Weekends with Vini*

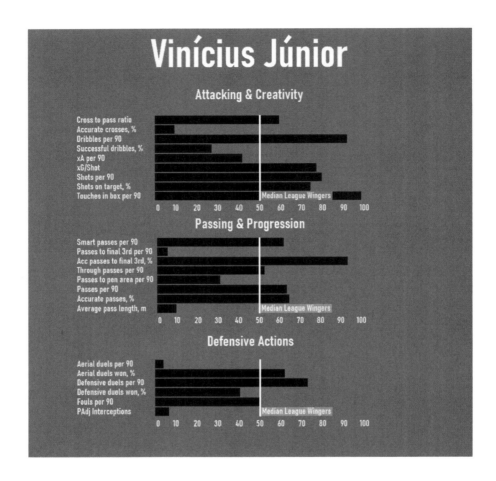

Vinícius Júnior's statistical profile is an interesting one. In each of the two attacking sections, you can see the dichotomy between his individual dynamism and his overall lack of efficiency. Capable of breaking the game open, he's also just as likely to botch the end product.

In his attacking and creativity section his two best percentile ranks were touches in the box and dribbles per 90 minutes. Only three players averaged more dribbles per 90 minutes than Vinícius Júnior's 8.86. Keep in mind that Dembélé only made five appearances, securing 372 minutes during the 2019/20 La Liga season. While there's no telling whether he would have kept that pace, Vini Jr's 29 appearances and 1,494 minutes played provides a more comprehensive picture of his season output.

One of the issues with his dribbling efficiency is that he's a right-footed player at left-forward who prefers to turn the corner on defenders. Typically, when you see an inverted forward, meaning a player who plays on the side of the field that's opposite their stronger foot, so a right-footed player on the left or vice versa, it's typical to see the player cut to the inside, be it on the dribble or while looking for his shot.

Vinícius has shown a preference to go around defenders on the outside. As he makes the move, the ball is still on his right foot. What that means is that he's showing the ball to the defender. If he was more proficient at dribbling with his left foot, he could use it to push the ball past the defender and engage in the dribble. In doing so, he increases the distance from the defender to the ball while also keeping his body between the two.

Instead, we see him keep the ball on his right foot, which gives defenders easy access to the ball.

As a thought experiment, I separated his stats by left and right-forward roles. My initial assumption was that a right-footed player who prefers to dribble past opponents on the outside with his right foot would greatly outperform his marks on the left side.

To my surprise, Vinícius Júnior had 66 successful dribbles out of 136 on the left, a 49% dribbling success rate. While playing on the right, he had three successful dribbles on 11 attempts. A surprisingly low 27% success rate.

The discrepancy in his dribbling success rate could very well be down to the fact that he is more comfortable playing on the left. That's where he generally plays and he's more accustomed to dribbling at defenders from that side of the pitch. Whether it's a positional orientation problem, a lack of success against particularly skilled defenders (he only registered 99 minutes at right-forward), or decision-making from the right side, there's an initial impression that he's better suited to the left. Should he receive more minutes at right-forward, it's hard to believe those numbers wouldn't improve, but experience in the position and readjusting how he engages would be key.

Regardless of which side he's playing on, one thing that most improved is his decision making. Watching Vinícius Júnior, there are certainly times where you wonder if he has a plan or if he's just dribbling to see how far he can progress the ball. He might beat the first player, but he doesn't show the greatest awareness of cover defenders, so will often lose out on the dribble to the cover defender or find himself forcing a bad pass as the defense collapses around him.

That's especially problematic on those occasions when he does cut inside from the left. Although it puts him on a stronger foot, he needs to show an awareness that, in the time it's taken him to complete the dribble, the defense has recovered their ground and positioned themselves centrally. As defenses close down, the space around him becomes more compact. Once the defense has organized, there has to be an awareness that the dribble either needs to stay on the outside or abandoned altogether.

This is where match context is so important. The best dribblers identify when they're engaged in a true 1v1, when there is space behind the defender, how far away the covered defender is, and what they hope to accomplish through the dribble. The dribble is an incredible tool for progression. Beating one player can throw the opposition into utter chaos, but it's so important to identify when the dribble is on. If it's not, it's best to help the side simply keep possession and look to construct a dribbling opportunity at a later time.

In terms of his attacking third efficiency issues, none is more glaring than his goal contributions versus expected goal contributions. With an xG of 4.48 and an xA of 1.58, Vinícius managed just three goals and one assist. Granted, he can't be blamed for his teammates slightly underperforming when Vinícius created scoring opportunities for them, but, the expectations for a forward at Real Madrid, especially on the left-side, would lead you to think one goal contribution every 373.5 minutes, or an expected contribution every 246.53 minutes, leaves much to be desired.

From a statistical standpoint, his 47% dribbling success rate and 22.92% accuracy on his 2.89 crosses P90 represent the greatest causes for concern. His dribbling efficiency rates just below the 30th percentile among La Liga forwards, while his crossing accuracy is nearly bringing up the rear, factoring into the 10th percentile.

His low accuracy percentage on crosses certainly gives the ol' hit and hope impression. That, combined with his 33% underperformance in xG, shows the efficiency issues with the final pass and shot.

It's certainly odd, because if you watch clips from Real Madrid's training sessions, Vini Jr's accuracy was typically quite impressive. His shots, in particular, are not only consistently good, but he also hits the occasional spectacular shots, absolute bangers. It does make you wonder if, as a young player donning the heavy badge of Real Madrid on his chest, he simply hasn't adapted to the pressures of playing for a global giant. Given his age, only turning 20 in July of 2020, the lack of maturity is reasonable.

One area where Vinícius certainly deserves credit is in his contribution to the defensive side of the game. His role in the man-marking high-press is the reason for the low number of aerial duels and possession adjusted interceptions. He's simply not asked to engage in those actions very often.

He's very committed in the high-press, quickly transitioning to the counterpress if the ball is lost on his side of the field, then picking up his mark as the team forces the ball backward.

Once the opponent has played over the first couple lines of Real Madrid's defense, he's then very willing to backtrack and engage in deeper parts of the field. Among forwards his defensive duels per 90 is in the top 30th percentile.

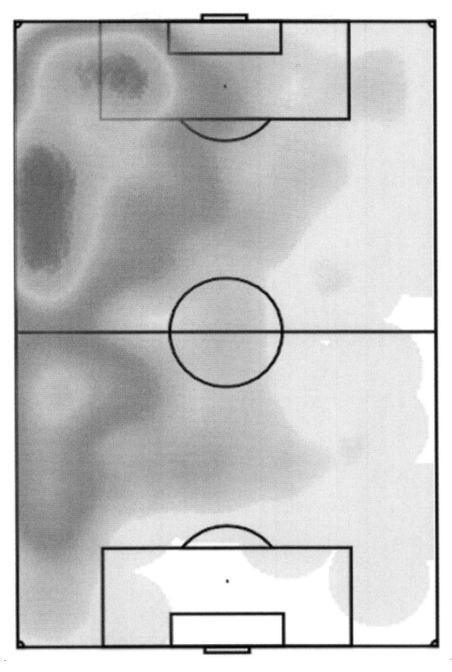

Turning to Vinícius' heat map, the lone bright spot in the defensive half of the pitch comes down to receiving the ball in counterattacking situations and his defensive contribution.

On the whole, he'll generally look to receive the ball in the entry to the final third. That's where his heat map shines brightest.

Notice how deep in the wing he prefers to receive. We've already discussed how he and Benzema play off of each other, with the Frenchman moving into the half space to pull defenders out of Vinícius Júnior's path. To increase the distance from the opposition's right-back to his cover defender, Vini will hug the touchline.

Once he receives the ball in that area, he'll look to make his run at the defender. If there's true isolation, a simple push past the defender with an oncoming sprint is what you'll most often see. Since he's got blazing pace, there's rarely much need for the step overs, scissors, flicks, and tricks.

If anything, he really only needs to add some deception to his shoulder feints. One thing you'll notice with struggling dribblers is that they frequently go into their move against the defender with the idea that a move is enough, that if done well the play will work out in their favor.

But 1v1s are ultimately battles of balance and timing. The defender is trying to force his attacker into taking the first action. If the attacker does so, the defender can then time his interaction and burst into action from a balanced state.

For attackers, the timing is based on the balance of the defender. He'll know it's time to engage once the defender's balance is compromised. The typical visual cues come from the hips, the activation of the quads, and the transference of weight from one foot to the other.

Once those visual cues emerge, elite dribblers know that the timing is right. They can then make their move with the defender in a compromised position.

Vinícius certainly has the desire and natural aggression of an elite dribbler, but improving his efficiency is key. That entails a great understanding of when the dribble is on, as well as reading the defender's balance cues and baiting imbalance.

When Vini wins his duel, you see the nice little pathway carved out on his heat map. He does tend to enter the box from the wing, roughly 6 to 12 yards from the endline. As he enters the box, he looks to make his next action in the left half space. It's from that point that he will either look to cut in his left towards the endline to send a negative pass or cut to his right to set up a shot or pass.

*Right-Sided Pairings*

I've already discussed Federico Valverde's right-sided work with some depth, so, just to quickly recap, Valverde's role on the right-hand side of the midfield was largely determined by his right-forward partner.

If Rodrygo, Gareth Bale, or Lucas Vázquez were in the game, Valverde was often utilized as a support player in the midfield. Playing in a more standard midfield role limits his dynamic runs forward, but the team usually finds a way to target him during counterattacks.

If he can get behind the opposition's midfield and the forwards are stretching the verticality of the field, forcing the backline into a retreat, space opens up for Valverde to run at the backline, pin a defender, and then slip a ball to a teammate.

If Isco starts on the right, his free role cues Valverde's actions. As Isco moves into the right half space, his movement tells Valverde to take the wing. If Isco drops in to help with the build-out, he's signaling Valverde to push higher up the pitch.

When Modrić started at right-center mid, the forward was typically a more traditional winger. With the Croatian running the show on the right, there was no need for someone like Isco. The skill sets were redundant, so a true winger was preferred.

*The Why*

Zidane's high attacking pairs filled a couple of functions.

First, they generated superiorities higher up the pitch. The four superiorities were mentioned earlier in the book. At the very least, Madrid looked to establish a qualitative superiority. Even if they were 2v2 in the wings on either side of the pitch, there was the assumption that their two could outplay the opposition's two.

Depending on how quickly Real Madrid moved the ball into the wings, there was the possibility of a quantitative advantage as well. With at least one player in the wing, a second in the half space, and oncoming support from the outside-back, Real Madrid looked for 2v1 and 3v2 situations. If the numbers worked out in their favor, Los Blancos were quick and decisive in the attack. They wanted to push play while the odds were stacked so heavily in their favor.

The second benefit of the high, wide attacking pairs is that it gave Real Madrid press breaking targets. With Kroos and Ramos able to spray the ball to any part of the pitch, Real Madrid's positional play looked to create situations that allowed them to easily break the press.

*To the Drawing Board*

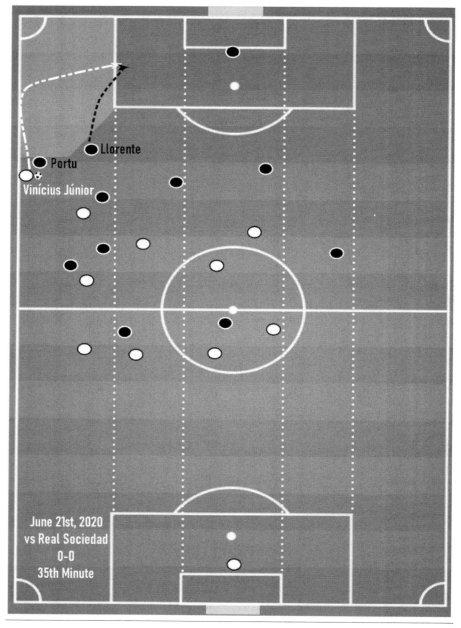

June 21st, 2020
vs Real Sociedad
0-0
35th Minute

In the June matchup against Real Sociedad, the utilization of attacking pairs was in full effect.

In this sequence, we saw Benzema drop into the midfield. Though his run wasn't picked up by the right-centerback, we saw Diego Llorente split his attention between covering for Portu and his Igor Zubeldia.

With the centerback not fully dedicated to covering the wing, Vinícius received the ball and immediately engaged in a 1v1 duel against Portu. A forward by trade, Portu lunged in with his tackle attempt. Vinícius Júnior easily skipped by him and sprinted deep into the wing.

As aggressively as Vinícius Júnior pursues the dribble, Benzema's off the ball movement is so important for the young Brazilian's success. Should the Frenchman stay higher up the pitch, his movement allows the backline to maintain their shape, putting them in a position to cover the outside-backs in 1v1 duels.

With Vinícius' tendency to move directly from one 1v1 duel to the next, opponents can bait him into the first dribble attempt when coverage is in place. If he wins the first duel, odds are the coverage defender is close enough to win the second.

The better the game Benzema had, typically, the better Vinícius Júnior played. The more an opponent had to focus on Big Benz, the more space was left for Vinícius.

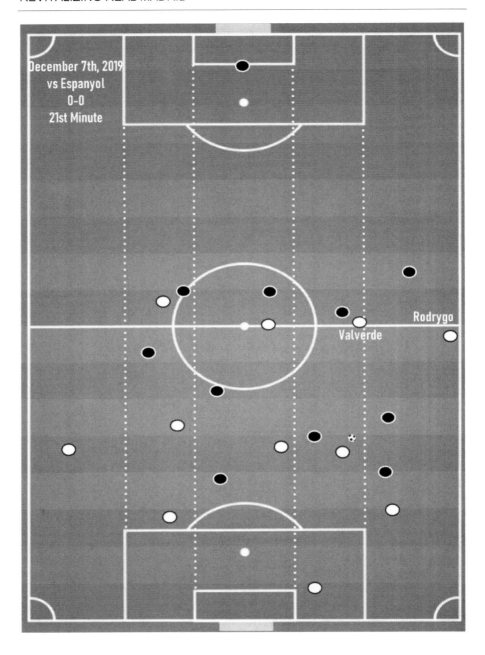

December 7th, 2019
vs Espanyol
0-0
21st Minute

Rodrygo

Valverde

Turning to a visual of the Valverde/Rodrygo relationship on the pitch, Rodrygo will typically be the wider of the two players, situating himself in the right-wing.

The Brazilian's presence in the wing means that Valverde will occupy the half space.

As the support midfielder, Valverde will generally play underneath Rodrygo. One of the objectives is to free Rodrygo to work his magic along the wings. Another is to offer pressure relief through a negative pass.

The other advantage of this relationship is that, with Rodrygo frequently taking his starting point on the right sideline and Benzema either in the central channel or left half space, gaps start to emerge in the backline. If space opens up between the opposing left and left-centerbacks, Valverde's pace allows him to attack that space without the possibility of the opponents recovering.

Depending on the state of the build-up, Valverde might leave his deeper midfielder role and push in line with his forward. From that higher starting point, he's creating space in the midfield if there's a necessity to drop or there's the possibility of simply staying up high to strengthen the wider attacking superiority.

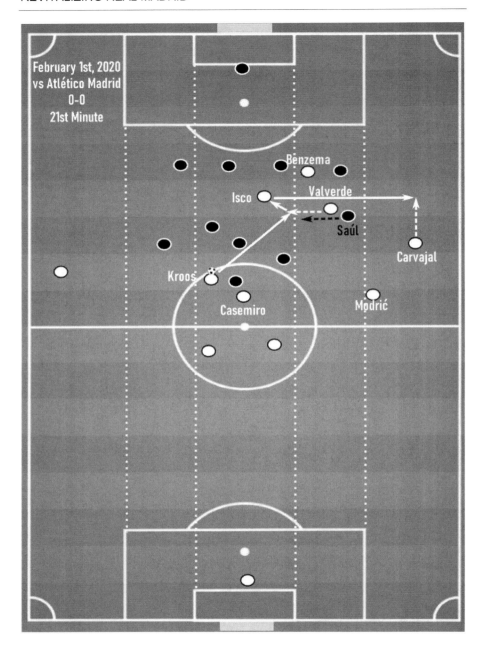

February 1st, 2020
vs Atlético Madrid
0-0
21st Minute

If Isco gets the start on the right, he and Valverde are essentially interchangeable.

The match against Atlético Madrid saw Isco play a free role, meaning that he's free to move about the field as he sees fit. If a gap opens up in the half space, the creative dynamo has the freedom to move into that space. If he identifies the possibility of linking up with Benzema centrally or even switching his positioning to the left side of the pitch, he's free to do so. As that free player, "free" meaning operating in a role outside of the team's larger picture tactics, his responsibility is to create unique attacking positions.

In this particular sequence, the advantage he tried to create was a central link up with Benzema. As Isco moved centrally, Valverde oscillated between the wing and half space. As Kroos' ball found Isco centrally, the Spaniard was joined by Benzema and Valverde in a central overload. With the opposition moving centrally to cover the new threat, the wing opened up for Carvajal's run.

Isco's simple square pass to Carvajal allowed the right-back to move into a crossing position while also serving to free the three players in the central overload to move into the box, giving Real Madrid a strong presence to meet the cross.

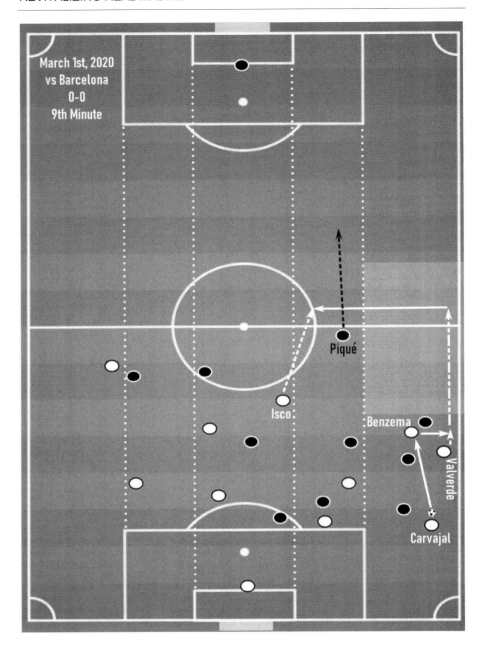

The attacking pairs were a tactical solution to create superiorities.

The benefits of the attacking pairs in this Real Madrid side, especially on the right side of the pitch when Isco was playing, was that he, Benzema, and Valverde could engage in positional switches to throw off the opposition.

When El Clásico came to Madrid in March, Isco moved high into the central channel as Benzema had dropped into midfield. With Isco filling the function of a #9 and Benzema dropping into the right-central midfielder's role, Valverde swapped roles with Isco, taking possession of the wing.

Carvajal picked out the checking run of Benzema and played to his center forward. Valverde was waiting in the wings ready to play off of Benzema's run. He corrected his starting point to both offer a passing lane to Carvajal and put himself in a position to play off of a potential Benzema pass.

When the ball arrived at Benzema's feet, he played a first-touch pass to Valverde in the wing. The young Uruguayan had loads of space in front of him and took a large first touch to attack it.

In the sequence, Valverde's midfielder instincts took over. Rather than running into the space that Barcelona had conceded, which, realistically, would have allowed him to at least enter the attacking third, if not the box, he played a central pass to Isco instead.

The pass was behind Isco which allowed the Barcelona midfield to recover and poke the ball away. Even though the sequence was not ultimately successful, the tactical look caught Barcelona by surprise. As mentioned, there was plenty of space for Valverde to run into. With his pace, it's unlikely a recovering defender would have caught him. As he continues to grow into the right-center midfield role in Madrid, especially if he's asked to play off of someone like Isco or Asensio, Valverde can be a real threat in the wings. He's not the most technical dribbler, but a simple push past the defender paired with a sprint in behind is all he needs.

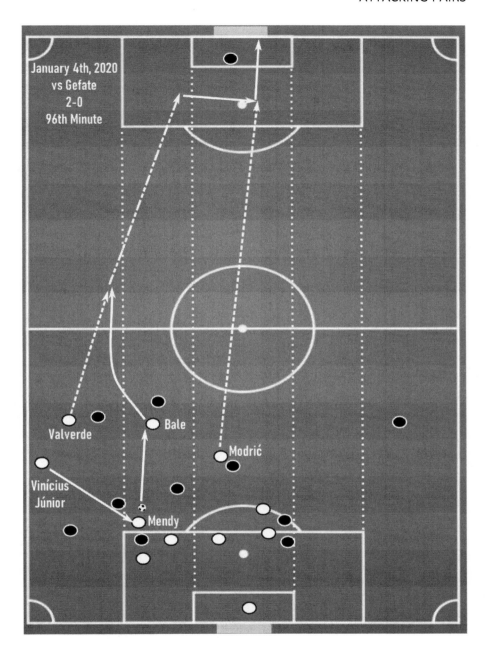

January 4th, 2020
vs Gefate
2-0
96th Minute

Valverde
Bale
Modrić
Vinícius
Júnior
Mendy

Late in a 3-0 road victory against Getafe, there was a great example of attacking pairs with an abnormal setup.

With Real Madrid defending deep in their defensive third while trying to close out the victory, Vinícius Júnior made a brilliant tackle on the left-wing, poking the ball free to Ferland Mendy. The Frenchman made a nice turn around his defender and played forward to Bale, who held off his defender and delivered an excellent bent pass into space for Valverde.

The Uruguayan easily beat his defender to the ball and dribbled unopposed into the box. With the keeper coming out to contest Valverde's lane to goal, Modrić made a hard run through the central channel. As Valverde decelerated, assessing whether he should take the shot or if he was better-suited playing into the path of an oncoming teammate, Modrić arrived in the box. He beat three Getafe players to the pass, slotting it into the empty net.

Even with Real Madrid defending deep in their own end, there's still the attacking pairs set up higher up the pitch.

With the two players situated close to each other, that gives Real Madrid high outlets, which is especially valuable in these transitional moments. Bale provides the outlet for the initial pass, but, because Real Madrid has Valverde connected to him in the wing, Bale's not asked to hold the ball under heavy pressure. Against a team like Getafe, holding up play against the last defender would likely have resulted in a firm whack to the legs or back.

Instead, Valverde gives Bale an option for the first touch pass. With Getafe aggressively pushing high up the pitch in pursuit of a goal, there's loads of space to run into. Pairing either Valverde or Vinícius Júnior on the left-side with Bale allows for the same results: a simple ball into space for the speedsters to chase down.

The attacking pairs in the wings give Real Madrid obvious targets while connecting a pass-first playmaker with a dynamic dribbler. They serve as the high targets in Real Madrid's attack and push the initiative into the final third and box.

That said, the pairing is typically just the starting point. As opponents recover their ground and the rate of progression is slowed, there are two other players that push up the field to help with the attack...the outside-backs.

*Chapter 13*

# Adapting the Outside-backs to the System

In terms of the outside-backs' attacking responsibilities, the expectations didn't change. Within Real Madrid's tactics, the outside-backs play prominent roles.

At times, they provide width, other times they make late runs to join the attack and they'll look to combine with the forwards and midfielders to accomplish the move to goal. They're highly involved in the attack and there's an expectation that they're among the team's most dynamic playmakers.

During the 2018/19 season, those expectations came back to haunt the team, moving the outside-back so high up the field that there was no chance of recovering during the opposition's counterattacks.

Zidane's work with the rest defense put the outside-backs in a position where they could fully commit to their attacking responsibilities without the fear of opponents attacking the spaces they vacated. If Marcelo or Ferland Mendy was highly involved in the attacking third, they knew Toni Kroos was in a position to cover for them. The rest defense adjustments afforded the highest players up the pitch the necessary freedom for success.

Between the left and right-backs, the left-sided player has historically been the more attack-oriented of the two, requiring the right-back to offer a more balanced approach.

Pairing with Marcelo since 2013, Dani Carvajal has handled that more balanced role to perfection. When healthy, he offers a level of consistency that's rare in the world's game. Fully committed to the defensive side of the game, but equally eager to push forward and join the attack, Carvajal's contribution to the team can sometimes go under the radar because he's strong across the board rather than world-class in one or two particular areas.

*Carvajal's Last Four Seasons by the Numbers*

Turning to Carvajal's radars over the past four seasons, you can pick out different trend lines in his and the team's performances. Remember that, like the Kroos radars, it's Carvajal's best statistical performances in each category that set the end values. For example, Carvajal's 0.17 xA during the 2016/17 season represents his best mark in the category over the previous four seasons, making it the high point of the radar.

# Dani Carvajal
## 2016/17

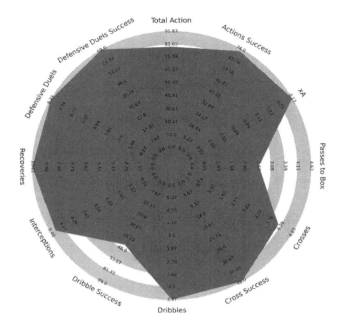

Taking a look at his 2016/17 performance, it was a fantastic season on both sides of the ball. In addition to setting the expected assist standard, his 69% defensive tools success rate, 8.71 defensive duels P90, 10.11 recoveries P90, 3.37 dribbles P90, and a 42% success rate on crosses were all high points over the 4 years.

His dribbling success rate and the number of passes he sent into the box were the only low points on the radar. Otherwise, it's hard to argue against this being a career year.

# Dani Carvajal
## 2017/18

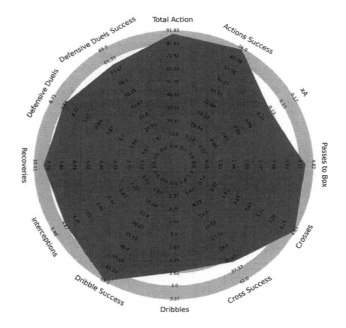

Moving on to 2017/18, different gaps emerge in the radar. Remember that in the final season with both Zinedine Zidane and Cristiano Ronaldo leading the team, the Frenchman had expressed concerns about the team's performance level and the need for reinvestment in personnel.

You can certainly see a drop in some significant categories. His xA of 0.13 is still fairly good, but Carvajal's dribble P90, as well as success rates in defensive duels and crosses also dropped. The regression in defensive duels success is the most worrisome of the four categories because of the more balanced role Carvajal plays within the team.

With regards to his dribbling and crossing contributions, the relationship between volume and success is significant. During this campaign, Carvajal engaged in fewer dribbles, but set a 4-year high in his success rate at 69%, which is spectacular. With his crosses, he set his four-year high with 4.83 P90, bringing his success rate down to approximately 33%.

As a general rule, when volume increases, success decreases. The actions might be less selective or more predictable, plus there are just more opportunities for failure. With that in mind, Carvajal's crossing and dribbling numbers are actually very respectable.

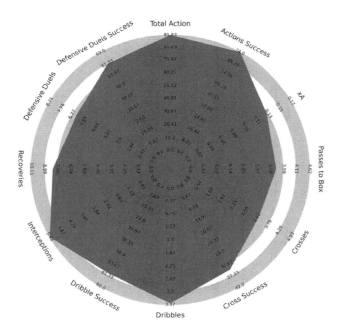

# Dani Carvajal
## 2018/19

Then we move to Zidane's gap year. Four-year highs in total actions, actions success percentage, and interceptions P90, as well as nearly equaling his dribbles P90 high, it's not so much that the radar has gaps. Rather, it gives the appearance of peaks.

While the regressions in all but four categories range from a reasonable drop-off to extreme underperformance, at least by Carvajal's high standards, it's important to remember that this was a down year for the team as well.

Without their beloved coach and the club's greatest ever player, it was a team trying to find its way. Their lost identity was really the cause of Zidane's return, so it would be unfair to pin Carvajal's 2018/19 regressions entirely on him.

# Dani Carvajal
## 2019/20

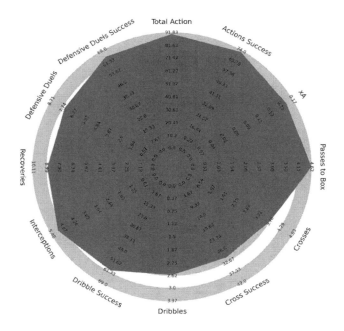

With Zidane back at the helm, Carvajal's performances made a significant recovery. Though he was a little less engaged with his crosses and dribbles, and ultimately less efficient with them, his numbers improved in nearly every other aspect.

Clarity of positional responsibilities certainly helps, as does the team's improved performance levels. While Carvajal only manages to set one high in one category, which is passes to the box P90 (4.62), most of his numbers aren't far from 4-year highs.

*Freedom for the left-back*

Shifting to the left side of the pitch, we'll now examine what the rest defense meant for the left-backs.

With Ferland Mendy arriving in the capital, the club was sending two messages.

First, they were actively looking for Marcelo's replacement. With the Brazilian entering the season at age 31, a long-term successor was needed. Outside-backs tend to see significant drops in performance around the age of 30, so it made sense for Pérez to look to the team's future. With Sergio Reguilón not convincing the critics in 2018/19, he was loaned to Sevilla for the 2019/20 season, then sold to Tottenham prior to the 2020/21 season with a buy-back clause inserted into the deal. That means that within a certain number of years, Real Madrid has the option to buy him back from Tottenham at a predetermined price.

The second reason for Mendy's signing was to improve the team defensively.

Given the history of attack first left-backs, signing Mendy as the long-term solution at left-back was a bit of a departure from tradition. He had put on excellent displays for Lyon during their Champions League games against Barcelona, but it goes without saying that he'll never add the attacking value of prime Marcelo.

What he does add is serviceable attacking in the left-wing, exceptional counterpressing, and reliable recovery runs to protect against counterattacks.

*Mendy's defensive work*

His defensive work was really spectacular in 2019/20. Rarely caught out of position, he was a key performer in both the counterpress and the man-marking high-press. Most significant of his defensive qualities are his excellent starting points, awareness of the imminent threats, and ability to cover ground in an instant.

One of the best defensive left-backs in the game, it's not that he puts up gaudy defensive numbers. Like most great defenders, his style is more preventative than direct.

From a statistical standpoint, he rated near the 70th percentile in aerial duels among La Liga outside-backs, but his defensive duels win percentage was just below the median and his possession adjusted interceptions fell below the 20th percentile. In terms of volume, his defensive duels per 90 minutes rated in the bottom 10% across the data set.

You might ask how an elite defensive player can produce such low marks in so many significant categories. After all, possession adjusted interceptions accounts for the fact that he has fewer opportunities than most outside-backs in defensive duels when percentage marks his tackling efficiency on a level playing surface.

The way Real Madrid's defensive tactics are set out, the press was most actively engaged in the attacking third of the pitch, leading primarily to middle third recoveries. Opponents tended to take their chances playing the long central aerial ball rather than the long diagonal out to the wings. So, the way the team's defensive tactics were applied led to fewer defensive actions from the outside-backs.

That's where you have to use the eye test to assess Mendy's season. Defensively, he offers a presence on the left-hand side that Real Madrid hasn't had in years. As the team counterpressed, he proved more than capable of either regaining possession for the team or, to recall the other objective of the counterpress, forcing the opposition to play backward.

*Mendy, room to grow in the attack*

The attacking side of his game was a little bit different. Among La Liga outside-backs he was one of the league leaders in dribbles P90. His dribble success rate hovered right around the 60th percentile and his touches in the box rated in the 75th percentile. Very active moving forward, he offered the side progressive runs down the left-wing.

However, Mendy's issues surrounded his efficiency and the quality of the final ball.

Despite playing 1,969 minutes, he only managed one goal on 0.09 xG.

Sure, you say, but he's an outside-back, aren't his assists tallies more important?

Yes, that is correct. In nearly 2,000 minutes, he managed just one assist on 0.93 xA. Contrast that to Carvajal's 5.18 xA for the season.

Additionally, while rating among the median of La Liga outside-backs with 3.2 crosses P90, his 28.57% crossing success rate was tied for 77th best at the position. So, you have moderate volume and below-average efficiency.

Higher up the pitch, his 1.28 touches in the box P90 rated 26th among his colleagues. Despite a reasonably high statistical performance in the category, it's shocking that he produced just 0.93xA. Remember that expected assists relate to the quality of the scoring opportunity the pass creates. So, even though Mendy was highly engaged in the attacking third, including in the box, there was very little end product.

Still reasonably young, entering the 2020/21 season at the age of 25, there's certainly a need for development in his attacking third contributions. Without that additional spark in the left-wing, Real Madrid will find it difficult to improve their 2019/20 goal production.

*Marcelo's revival*

The last outside-back we'll talk about is Marcelo, or in the words of legendary broadcaster Ray Hudson, "MARCELO, MARCELO, MARCELO."

It's impossible to deny that Marcelo's 2018/19 form was the precursor for the Mendy transfer. Losing his influence in attack and struggling to contribute in the defensive phases, he was a shadow of his former self.

Though the Mendy transfer and Marcelo's age show that the veteran has one foot out the door, 2019/20 saw his workload scaled back, which seemed to refresh the Brazilian. Whether that was his last hoorah or if he's got more in the tank, the Marcelo we saw in this title-winning season was enough to put a smile on every Madridista's face.

The beloved, playful club legend had a fantastic season. His possession adjusted interceptions rated in the 25th percentile and defensive duels in the bottom 10%, but he was remarkably efficient in those few duels that he did engage in, winning 72% of them. Among outside-backs with more than 1,000 minutes, only Santiago Arias of Atlético Madrid had a higher percentage.

We'll move on to the attacking set of things given that that's where Marcelo makes the biggest impact.

For the season, he rated in the 90th percentile or better in touches in the box, passes to the penalty area, smart passes, progressive passes, and passes, all on a per 90 basis. His efficiency numbers weren't far behind rating just outside of the 90th percentile in dribbling success percentage, passing accuracy, and accurate forward passes percentage.

He was also responsible for one of the biggest plays of the season. During the home leg of El Clásico, Barcelona managed to slip Messi behind the Real Madrid backline. Every spectator must have assumed that Messi would score his goal to give Barcelona the lead.

Then, out of nowhere, Marcelo made the recovery run of his career. He tracked Messi down and made a brilliant sliding tackle, saving the game and Real Madrid's season.

Down the stretch, he proved to be a vital rotational piece, serving as the left-back against teams that were expected to defend deep in their own end. His creativity and flair during the stretch run brought back memories of years past.

If that memorable season marks the end of his regular playing time at the club, and early matches during the 2020/21 campaign suggests that's the case, Madridistas can at least revel in his 2019/20 performances, his last hoorah.

*Marcelo vs Mendy*

Comparing Mendy and Marcelo's heat map, a few key differences stand out.

First, it's clear that Mendy was more active in the defensive half of the pitch. His map contains relatively hot spots in the left-wing just outside the box and continues all the way to midfield. Marcelo's heat map really only starts to light up near the entry to the middle third of the pitch.

Second, the Brazilian's heat map shows bright spots in the middle third, on either side of the midfield line, then lights up again in the attacking third.

With respect to his attacking third entry, there's more of an emphasis on entering the half space than you see in Mendy's map. Even though he's left-footed, Marcelo enjoys cutting inside to pin the opposition's defense and wreak havoc.

In contrast, Mendy tends to stay in the wing where he has more time and space to operate. He's not nearly as technical a player as Marcelo, so the additional time and space on the wing suits him well.

*To the Drawing Board*

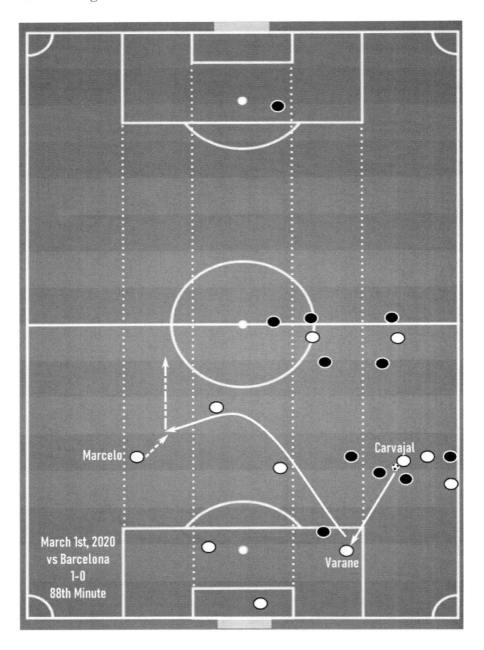

Speaking of that El Clásico game, that's where we'll turn for our first example of how the outside-backs fit into Zidane's tactics.

In this example, we have Real Madrid locked in a 3v4 situation on the right-wing with Dani Carvajal on the ball. With numbers favoring Barcelona, Real Madrid was desperate to play out of their pressure and switch the point of attack.

On the left side of the pitch, you can see Marcelo setting the team's left-sided width from deep in the left half space. He was certainly gambling. Had Barcelona recovered possession only three Real Madrid players were well-positioned to contest their path to goal, and Marcelo was not one of them.

Instead, he took a risk, trusting the players in the right-wing to play out of Barcelona's high-press.

It worked, Carvajal managed to pick out a negative pass to Varane who then bent a wonderful ball into the path of Marcelo.

The switch of play not only shows the press resistance of Carvajal and the distribution ability of Varane, but also the attack first approach Marcelo takes to the position. In matches where they needed that little bit of Marcelo magic or his big-game experience, the veteran slid into the lineup and produced.

In this example, his discipline to stay higher up the pitch left the switch on and placed him in a position to aggressively attack space, leading the charge up field.

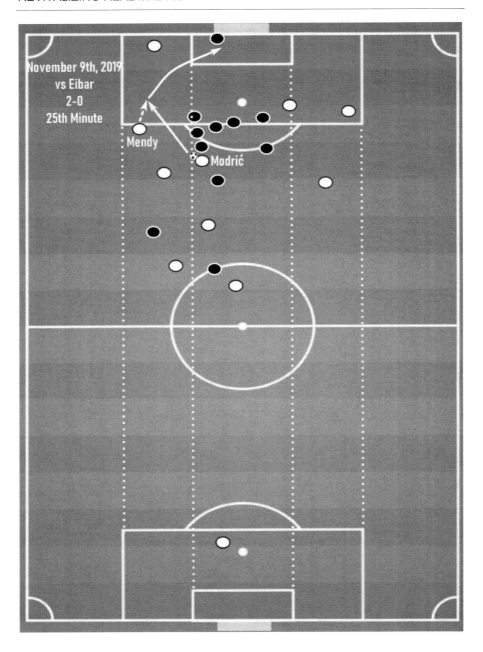

November 9th, 2019
vs Eibar
2-0
25th Minute

Mendy

Modrić

Roughly a third of the way into the season, Real Madrid traveled to the Basque Country for a matchup against Eibar. After a poor start to the season, earning just two points in the first five games, the home side entered this match with four wins and two draws in the previous eight games, including back-to-back wins against Villarreal and Leganés.

But it simply wasn't meant to be. Real Madrid pushed the hosts aside en route to a 4-0 win.

Midway through the first half, Mendy had one of his more typical box entries. Starting on the left-wing, Mendy saw Luka Modrić in possession and looking to deal. With Eibar centrally concentrated, the half space was wide open for Mendy's run.

He burst onto the scene, latching onto a well-weighted pass from Modrić.. The Frenchman identified his numbers at the far post and attempted to play the ball in their direction.

Unfortunately, his cross was mis-hit, flying securely into the hands of the goalkeeper, Marko Dmitrović. The sequence perfectly encapsulated the type of arrival most used by Mendy, the area of the box that he targeted as a crossing location, and a reminder of the work to be done with his deliveries.

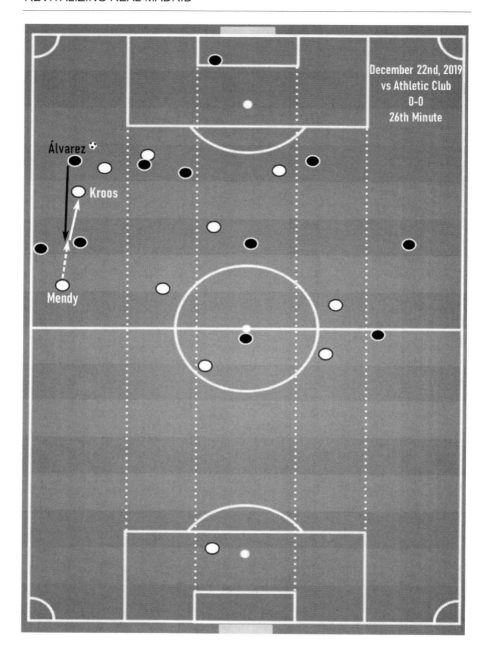

Again, while the final product is a bit of an issue for Mendy, he's so reliable in the defensive phases of the game, particularly in the high-press.

When Real Madrid hosted Athletic Club, Yeray Álvarez had possession of the ball in his right-wing. Kroos stepped up to apply pressure with the players behind and beside him already set in their man-marking scheme.

Álvarez had two options on the play. The first was to play back to the goalkeeper, Unai Simón.

The second, which he ultimately decided on, was to try and direct play down his wing. With his teammates 2v1 against Mendy higher up the wing, a successful pass to one of the two would allow them to combine around Mendy.

Mendy read the pass beautifully. As Álvarez attempted to pick out his teammates, Mendy confidently stepped forward to reclaim possession for Real Madrid.

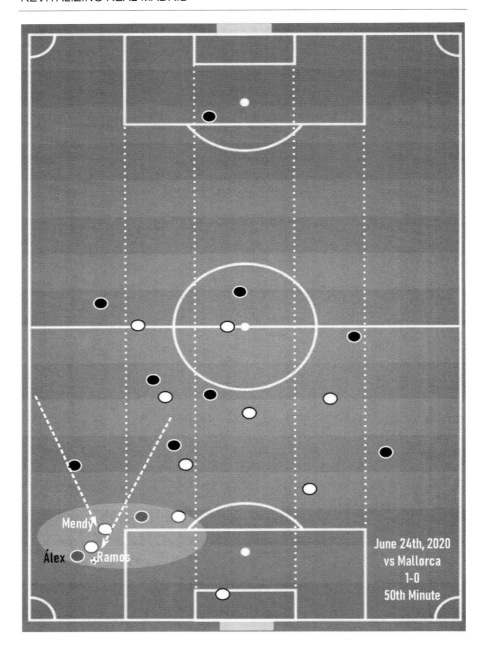

June 24th, 2020
vs Mallorca
1-0
50th Minute

The last area to highlight is the way Sergio Ramos and Mendy worked off of each other in their defensive third.

Back on June 24th, Mallorca managed to play Álex behind Mendy, calling Ramos into duty. The two players seamlessly switched roles with Ramos assuming the responsibilities of the first defender and Mendy sliding centrally in coverage of Ramos.

With the Frenchman in coverage, Ramos could afford to be more aggressive on the play. He engaged Álex knowing that any passes or dribble into the half space would end with a Mendy recovery.

One additional note is how well Real Madrid covered on this play. Beyond Ramos and Mendy, you also see Varane sliding into the left half space to offer coverage to the nearest passing option, as well as Carvajal dutifully making his recovery run on the far side, securing the middle and cutting out the possibility of a back post run. It's a level of commitment that the backline struggled to achieve the previous season. With the outside-backs, especially Mendy and a refreshed Marcelo, committing to the defensive cause, there were far fewer gaps for opponents to attack in Real Madrid's final third.

## Chapter 14

# The Midseason Slump

If you were asked to break Real Madrid's 2019/20 season into three performance blocks, where would you break up the season?

Taking notes on the season's results and performance measures, here's my submission.

*First phase: A Hot Start*

Our first period ranges from round 1 to 15. The final game in the sequence is a 2-0 victory against Espanyol.

Between La Liga and the Champions League, Real Madrid played 21 matches, averaging 2.14 goals per 90 minutes, 1.99 xG P90, and holding the opposition to 0.97 xG P90. They also managed 16.77 shots per game, 6.91 of which hit the target. In La Liga play, they recorded 10 victories, 4 draws, and a loss to Mallorca. Those 34 points equated to 2.27 points per game.

During that time frame, Benzema made appearances in all 21 matches, scoring 16 goals, good for an average of 0.77 P90. Other stats on a per 90 basis include 0.73 xG, 0.29 assists, 4.02 shots, and 1.74 shots on target.

He was on fire in the opening months of the season.

Then Hazard picked up his ankle injury and opponents adjusted to Madrid's tactics.

*Second Phase: The Slump*

For whatever reason, Real Madrid don't enjoy their trips to Estadio de Mestalla. Valencia often find success when they host Real Madrid in their home stadium. Despite an up and down season that saw Valencia finish with a -7 goal differential, they managed to secure a 1-1 draw against Zidane's men.

If the dropped points were the worst thing to come out of this draw, the match would have simply been a blight in an otherwise strong campaign. However, for whatever reason, Real Madrid seemed to spiral into a bizarre funk.

Yes, the next match was a 0-0 draw against their arch-nemesis, followed by another 0-0 draw against Athletic Club, then five victories. Looking beyond the facade of performance underlined by victories, something wasn't right in Madrid.

From December 15th, 2019 until March 8th, 2020, the club's last game before the COVID-19 suspension of play, Real Madrid managed six wins, four draws, and two losses in 12 La Liga matches. Those 22 points come out to 1.83 points per game, a 0.44 decline.

Real Madrid's goals per game dropped to 1.42, slightly worse than their 1.47 xG P90.

One of the reasons for the team's declining performance was Karim Benzema's personal slump. After grabbing a goal against Valencia, he went on to score just twice in his next 12 games (all competitions), a 0.17 P90 average.

It's not as though he was wildly underperforming his xG. During that same period, his xG was a measly 3.78, a 0.32 P90 average.

To make matters worse, he wasn't creating for teammates either, registering just one assist over that time frame.

So what went wrong?

Statistics tell us that he was less involved in the team's moves to goal. He went from averaging just over four shots P90 to just 2.47.

On film, it seems like Benzema was spending more time in deeper, playmaking roles. He's always had a preference to drop into the half spaces to facilitate play, especially on the left-hand side, but these movements were becoming deeper and deeper. At times it seemed like he was dropping unnecessarily deep, then not having enough time to get back into the box to get on the end of service. As a service dependent player, those deep runs can help him enter the box untracked but, if the timing is off, it leaves him with few opportunities to goal.

Another influence was the absence of Eden Hazard. From mid-December to the March 8th, 2020 match against Real Betis, the Belgian managed just two appearances, starts against Celta de Vigo and Levante.

Prior to the COVID-19 suspension of play, Real Madrid had an xG of 29.42 when Hazard played, which comes out to a 1.95 xGP 90. That even includes his slow start to the season. If you look at his 11 matches prior to the pause in league play, Madrid recorded a 27.42 xG with him in the lineup, a 2.49 P90 average. Those are elite numbers that remind Madridistas of years past. When he played he was hugely influential and part of that comes down to his relationship with Benzema. The pair managed to get the best out of each other, a skill no one else managed.

When Isco played, he was virtually a fourth midfielder, which put the wing attacking burden on the outside-back. We've just discussed Mendy's issues with the final ball. During that stretch, he started six games and made three other appearances, chipping in with two assists. Marcelo picked up five starts, scoring a goal and adding two assists during that time.

For his part, Isco played 576 minutes during that mid-season slump, adding just one goal on 0.72xG. To make matters worse, as a left-forward, he only added eight shots with four making it to the target.

If it wasn't Isco playing on the left, it was most likely Vinícius Júnior, who garnered 456 minutes during the team's slump. Again, just one goal and no assist. Like Isco, his xG was low, registering at just 1.47, a 0.29 P90 average.

The additional issue we saw with the Vini Jr/Big Benz partnership was the lack of synchronicity. Benzema's frequent midfield drops created better attacking conditions for Vinícius Júnior, often setting him up for a 1v1 against his opponent. However, that came with a cost, with Benzema in midfield and Vinícius Júnior blazing a trail into the box, the Frenchman had issues getting into the box to arrive at the end of a Vinícius Júnior delivery. There was a tendency from the youngster to force the issue when he arrived in or near the box, at times showing a lack of maturity and understanding. Even though he was in a position to send the final ball, his teammates weren't ready to receive.

While he did offer a truer left-forward presence when on the pitch, at least in comparison to Isco, part of playing left-forward at Real Madrid is understanding how to play off of Benzema.

*To the Drawing Board*

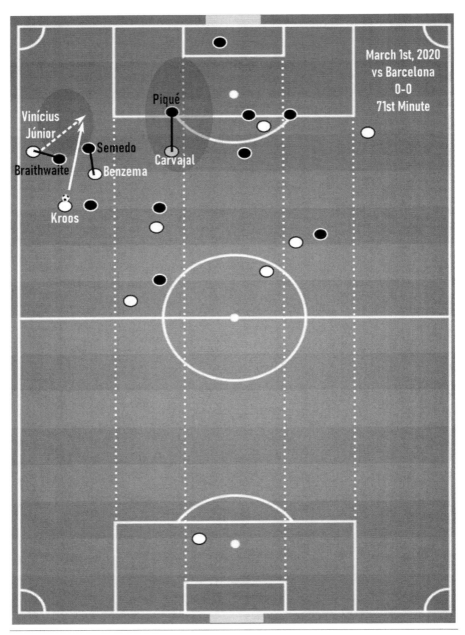

Vinícius Júnior
Braithwaite
Semedo
Benzema
Carvajal
Piqué
Kroos

March 1st, 2020
vs Barcelona
0-0
71st Minute

In the game-winning goal against Barcelona at the Estadio Santiago Bernabéu, we got a glimpse of what the Vinícius Júnior/Benzema partnership can look like.

The focus here is the manner in which Real Madrid's attackers occupy Barcelona's defenders. Though Benzema initially started closer to the center near Piqué, he dropped into the half space, but the veteran defender didn't bite. To ensure Piqué did not slide further towards Real Madrid's left-sided overload, Dani Carvajal, whose run had taken him more centrally to switch places with Valverde, forced his Spanish international teammate to stay close to the central channel. That left Nélson Semedo responsible for Benzema and Martin Braithwaite for Vinícius Júnior.

When the relationship is working, Benzema's half space checks, or wing in this case, creates running room for Vinícius behind the backline. Benzema's deep checks into midfield also serve to take away the cover defender, so, with Braithwaite guarding Vini Jr, Semedo would ideally have dropped behind his teammate to deny running space to the Brazilian.

However, with Benzema drawing Semedo towards him, Kroos signals for Vinícius' run and plays a perfectly weighted through ball.

The rest is history.

With Piqué forced to play the balancing act of removing the option to Carvajal while also narrowing Vinícius Júnior's angle to goal, the Brazilian managed to get the deflected goal off of the big Spaniard.

If Vinícius was consistently finishing off his chances, Benzema's deep drops wouldn't have such a negative impact on the team's co-production. However, since Vini Jr did struggle to cap off of plays and Benzema was pulled away from the box, the lack of timing and understanding between the two reduced the goal-scoring threat from the left-hand side of the pitch.

*No Secondary Goal-Scorers*

## Player xG During 12-Game Mid-Season Slump

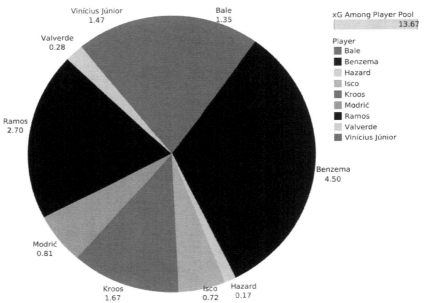

Another reason for the goals drying up was the lack of secondary scorers. The pie chart shows the xG of the forwards, midfielders (minus Casemiro), and Sergio Ramos during the 12-game span from the Valencia to Real Betis games.

Adding the game against Valencia to the mix helps Benzema's total, but, even still, 4.5 xG over 12 games isn't great, especially when penalty kicks are factored in.

The other player taking the team's penalty kicks, Ramos, boasts the second-highest total at 2.70. Penalty kicks carry an expected goals value of 0.76 on Wyscout, the data source for this book. Benzema and Ramos took one penalty kick apiece during the mid-season slump, converting their chance. By reducing their listed xG values by 0.76, you then have their non-penalty expected goals (NPxG), which gives a better sense of open play and set piece goal-scoring opportunities.

Looking at the other totals in the chart, Vinícius Júnior, Gareth Bale, and Toni Kroos were the only other players to register an xG above one.

Keep in mind that this is over a 12-match stretch. When the club desperately needed someone to step up during Benzema's drought, Ramos, the centerback, was the player with the highest xG, with or without the penalty.

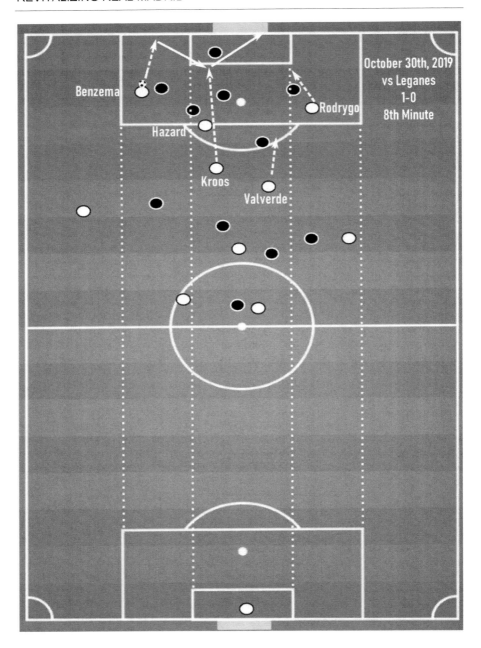

Prior to the slump, we saw a really nice example of a goal from a secondary scorer just before the slump when Real Madrid took on Leganes.

Benzema picked up the ball on the left, then proceeded to dribble into the box. With Benzema pushed out to the left, Hazard switched roles with him, moving into the central channel. The Belgian stopped near the top of the 18, which caused the centerbacks to pause momentarily. The passing lane to Hazard was blocked and there was coverage in the gap between Hazard and the goal.

With the centerbacks focusing exclusively on Hazard, Kroos sprinted between the two centerbacks. His run into the box was timed to perfection as he waited for Benzema to make his initial movement towards the endline. Once Benzema made his move, he played a negative pass to the six. Kroos arrived just in the nick of time to complete the sequence with a goal.

From a tactical perspective, the first talking point is Hazard switching roles with Benzema, giving Real Madrid a central presence. Hazard is committing two defenders to the same area. With the two players switching roles, Hazard, although he's not making a deep run into the box, at least occupies the two centerbacks.

That allows for the second tactical point, which is the run of Kroos. Starting from a deeper position, his run was untracked by the backline until it was too late to stop him. He also did brilliantly to read Hazard's positioning at the top of the box. Since the Belgian was occupying the centerbacks, keeping them away from the 6-yard box, Kroos read the opportunity and burst into the gap.

Finally, we have Rodrygo's positioning at the far post. It may seem like a small detail, possibly inconsequential to the goal itself, but with Rodrygo attacking the far post, he commits his mark to defending against him. Since the defender is stuck marking Rodrygo at the far post, he's unable to slide centrally, allowing the centerbacks to become more compact and deny space to Kroos. It's a small detail, but one that indirectly contributes to this goal.

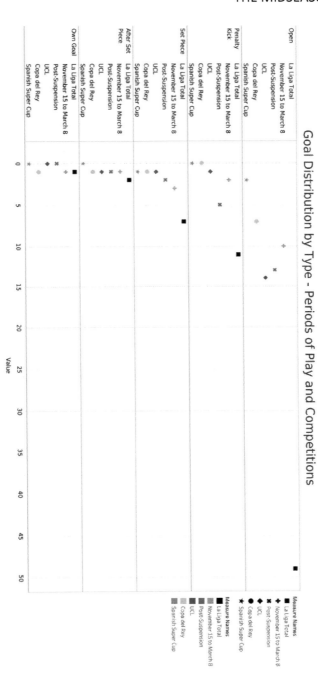

Goal Distribution by Type - Periods of Play and Competitions

With the well of open play goals seemingly run dry, Real Madrid became more dependent on set piece and penalty kicks. Of the 17 goals they scored from December 15th, 2019 to March 3rd, 2020, a span of 12 La Liga matches, only 10 goals were from open play. Of the other goals, one was an own goal, another came immediately after a set piece, three arrived through set pieces, and the last two from penalty kicks.

Referencing the goal distribution by type chart, the run of play from November 15th to March 8th is the only measure where the open play goals are lower than the number of games played.

So not only were Real Madrid struggling to score goals, they had become dependent on clean sheets and goals from outside of open play.

It's worth mentioning the team's stellar defensive work during this difficult period of play. Over those 12 games, Real Madrid conceded just eight goals, a per game average of 0.67. The xGA wasn't far behind either as they allowed just 0.80 per 90 minutes.

As the team had issues finding the net, they leaned heavily on one of Europe's strongest defenses. Despite the struggles to consistently produce goals, Zidane's tactics paved a new path for Real Madrid's success. Rather than outscoring the opponents in high-scoring affairs, this side took pride in their defensive performances. Throughout the season, you could see the team celebrating blocked shots, recovery runs, and fantastic saves from Courtois. They became a team that found joy in their defensive achievements.

Every team goes through rough patches over the course of a season. Madrid will certainly be unhappy with the points they dropped during this slump, but key wins against Barcelona, Atlético Madrid, Sevilla, and Getafe gave them some breathing room. Even with some unfortunate results and poor performances, the team managed to tread water until the suspension of play.

And that's where we enter the third phase of the season.

## Chapter 15

# Third Phase: The Post-COVID-19 Surge

Several of the top clubs entered the COVID-19 suspension of play with a sigh of relief and it must be said Real Madrid was among that number. Coming off of a disastrous loss against Real Betis, the side was wounded, visibly fatigued, and in need of a restart. Their play was uninspiring, short on solutions and missing key players, especially Hazard. To make things worse, the March 8th loss to Real Sociedad put Real Madrid two points behind Barcelona, leaving the La Liga crown out of their control, at least temporarily.

During the mid-season slump, Zidane and the club knew the defensive tactics were good enough to help them secure some difficult points and catch Barcelona. It was the other side of the ball that needed help. The difficulty was to find the balance in correcting the attacking tactics without hurting the team defensively.

After 98 days, Real Madrid returned to the pitch with a 3-1 win over Eibar. It was by no means a perfect performance as Eibar held Madrid to six shots while having 11 of their own, putting three goals past the away side was a massive step in the right direction.

Adding to the positives, Eden Hazard returned to the pitch after his long layoff, collecting an assist while playing 63 minutes.

Three days later, the team received another boost when Marco Asensio returned from an ACL injury. Within seconds of stepping onto the field, he used his first touch in over a year to score the second goal of the game. He'd also go on to assist Benzema's second goal in the 86th minute.

With those two players back in the fold, the number of possible lineups and rotations Zidane could plan increased. There was also the added benefit of fitting Hazard and Benzema into the same lineup.

When Asensio played, he gave Real Madrid something different on the right-hand side. Skilled like a midfielder but with the nose for goal of a forward, Asensio's return from injury both helped his team keep the opponents off balance and gave them another player who could put the ball in the net. In nine appearances, all during the stretch run, Asensio managed to score three goals and add one assist.

Let's take a deeper look at what Asensio's role looked like.

*To the Drawing Board*

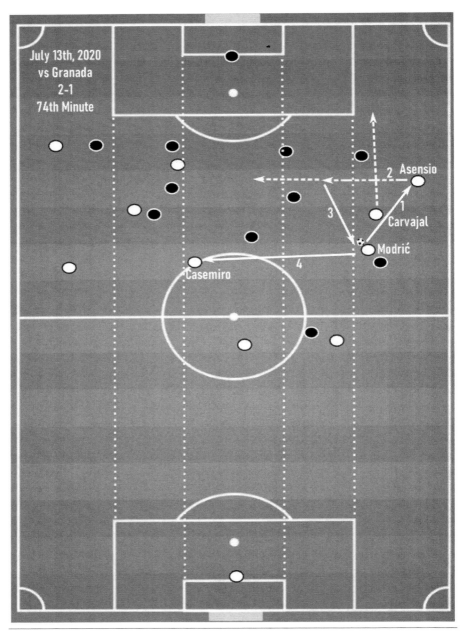

July 13th, 2020
vs Granada
2-1
74th Minute

2 Asensio

1 Carvajal

3

Modrić

4

Casemiro

In a hard-fought 2-1 win over a very impressive Granada side, Asensio came into the game for the last 32 minutes. In his nine appearances, only three were starts, so he did fill the function of a super sub. This game was no different.

Since Modrić was the right-center attacking midfielder at the time, you could argue Carvajal was a player most naturally suited to provide width on the right side of the pitch.

In the sequence, Asensio starts wide, which is something that stood out in the film. He did have a tendency to take up a wider starting point in the middle third of the field before moving centrally as the team entered the final third. One reason is to give the team another body in the box. He's not much of an aerial threat, but he reads crosses and lanes for negative passes very well, allowing him to be in the right place at the right time. He's also got an incredible shot from distance. If that's news to you, make some popcorn, plop onto a comfortable chair, and find a highlight reel.

In order to create space centrally, he likes to take a wide starting point so that he's not tipping off defenders about the space he's trying to create.

In the 74th minute against Granada, Real Madrid established a numeric superiority in the right-wing. Granada quickly closed down the space, but couldn't prevent Real Madrid from playing out of pressure.

Modrić passed to Asensio, who dribbled into the right half space. Once there, he was pressured again by the Granada defense and set the ball back to Modrić. As Modrić played into the feet of Casemiro, Asensio continued his run into the central channel.

Much like Isco, the Asensio role came with the freedom to move about the pitch. As the free man in the formation, it was his responsibility to identify pockets of space, form superiorities, and create goal-scoring opportunities.

Real Madrid always has a target on their back, especially in La Liga. To complicate matters further, once they passed Barcelona in the standings, opponents saw each game as a way to spoil the season.

Knowing that his side would see the very best in each opponent, Zidane had to prepare them for the tactics they were likely to encounter and guide them through possible solutions. Having Asensio and Hazard back in the lineup, at least for the most part, helped him diversify the tactical approach, but there were still some match up specific tactics to employ.

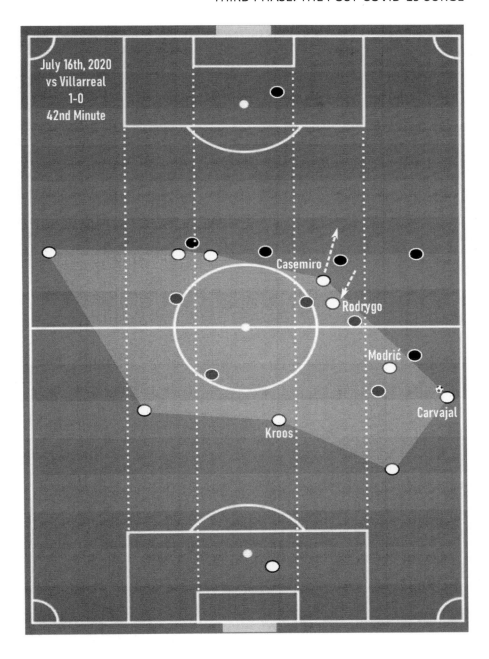

July 16th, 2020
vs Villarreal
1-0
42nd Minute

Casemiro

Rodrygo

Modrić

Carvajal

Kroos

One of the more interesting attacking tactics after the return to play was Real Madrid's build-out approach against Villarreal.

We've already discussed how Real Madrid used the build-out as a means of preparing to attack the opponent. As they circulate the ball among the deepest players, they're looking for specific cues from the opposing team. Once those cues arrive, they know the timing is right to launch the attack.

Against Villarreal, we saw that after Real Madrid beat the initial high-press, the away side was content to drop their numbers behind the ball and defend in the middle block.

Rather than butting heads with the compact block, Madrid frequently dropped Kroos between the two centerbacks, pushed Casemiro high up the pitch, and gave Modrić the freedom to drop in when he felt necessary.

In this particular sequence Rodrygo, who started high and wide, dropped into the right half space. Casemiro, who is stationed higher up the pitch anyway, saw the checking run of Rodrygo and offered a run behind the backline. Carvajal didn't pick up his run, but emptying the midfield and moving Casemiro higher up the pitch was a tactic Real Madrid turned to throughout the game.

That does relate to a previous point about Casemiro leaving the build-up, switching roles with Modrić to allow the more press-resistant Croatian to help the team out of trouble.

*Rotations*

The return of Hazard and Asensio gave the club a massive boost in their title bid. With games planned every 3 or 4 days, rotations were necessary. Clubs that didn't implement a rotation struggled during the stretch. Rust impacted many teams in the opening few matches, then fatigue kicked in as many players were not fully prepared for the restart of the season.

Over the final 11 games, the most difficult opponents on Real Madrid's schedule included Real Sociedad, Getafe, Athletic Club, Granada, and Villarreal. All good teams, but the collection still gave Madrid a better remaining schedule than Barcelona.

Their Catalonian rivals still had to play Sevilla, Athletic Club, Atlético Madrid, and Villarreal. The games against Sevilla and Atlético Madrid were especially tricky. The two teams not only qualified for the Champions League, but they also finished the return to play without a single loss between them. Loads of draws, nine to be exact, two of which came against Barcelona, one for each team, but no losses.

Over the final 11 games of the season, Barcelona dropped 9 out of 33 points. By contrast, Real Madrid only dropped two. Their draw came in the final game of the season against Leganés with the La Liga title already secured. The only impact the game had on the final standings was in giving Barcelona the appearance of a tighter title race.

*Grinding out results*

After months in quarantine and with little time to prepare for the restart, sloppiness was expected across the league. While the standard of play wasn't poor, the inconsistencies seemed more prevalent.

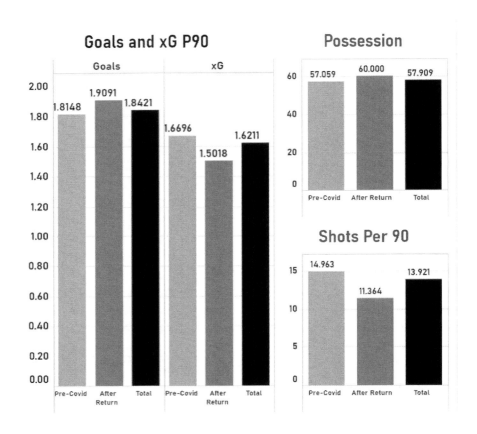

Real Madrid was no exception. The attacking dashboard shows four key attacking stats in relation to their pre-COVID suspension marks as well as the season total.

Looking at goals per 90 minutes, the 1.91 mark exceeds both the pre-COVID and total statistics for the season. However, when you move from real to expected goals, Real Madrid either had more luck or better finishing in the final 11 games of the season. With an xG P90 total of 1.50, there was a drop off in the quality and number of scoring opportunities.

Looking at shots per 90, their tally after the return to play rated well below the pre-COVID and total season numbers. In fact, in six of the final 11 games, Real Madrid recorded 10 shots or fewer.

That all came with their highest possession percentage. At 60%, there's a slight increase in the category. But, as the saying goes, it's not how much possession you have, it's what you do with it.

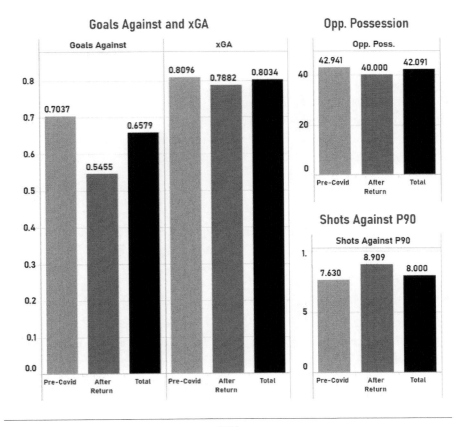

With just 40% possession on average, Real Madrid's opponents also produced some odd stat lines.

8.91 shots per game is an objectively low total, but it still beat out the pre-COVID and total season shots against stats P90.

However, even with the increase in shots, opponents still struggled to produce quality opportunities. Over the final 11 games of the season, opponents averaged 0.79 xG per 90 minutes. That amounts to a 0.09 xG per shot, hinting at low-quality shooting opportunities.

Even worse, they only averaged 0.55 goals per game. So, not only did they have a few opportunities, but they were also of a low standard and the execution was even worse.

Considering Real Madrid's attacking and defensive stats, it seems only fair that their defensive work was the key to reclaiming the crown. Despite bringing in Hazard and Jović, Madrid only managed to score 70 goals on the season. Think back to the Cristiano Ronaldo years and anything below 100 was seen as a disappointment.

Without those video game numbers, Real Madrid had to find a new way to win.

Zidane found that through his tactical innovations. With the team experiencing an identity crisis, Zidane's return introduced new tactical concepts, at least new in relation to the club, and rebuilt this team from a secure defensive foundation.

Additionally, his guidance and mentality in such a bizarre year were game-changers. Given the number of points La Liga's other top teams dropped during the stretch run, Madrid's mentality was the difference-maker. They had to grind out some difficult victories, but the players channeled the pressure into title-winning performances.

# Chapter 16

# Celebrating 34

As the final whistle sounded on July 16th, 2020, Real Madrid players, coaches, and executives began their celebrations.

Number 34 belongs to Real Madrid, ending Barcelona's two-year reign.

As the club and fans celebrated the title, albeit in a socially distanced manner, 2020's disappointments and hardships faded into the periphery. The suspension of play made everyone wait a little bit longer, but, given what the world has endured during this incredibly challenging year, the title was that much sweeter for the club and fans.

*La Liga Goal Distribution*

La Liga Goal Distribution

Open
49
70%

Penalty Kick
11
16%

Set Piece
7
10%

After Set Piece
2
3%

Own Goal
1 – 1%

Recapping Real Madrid's goals, breaking them down by type, they finished the season with 49 goals from open play, accounting for 70% of their total production.

Next up were the penalty kicks. With 11 for the season, penalties earned a 16% goal share. They were especially valuable in the return from the COVID-19 suspension of play. On a few occasions, when the opponent had frustrated and rebuffed Madrid's attempts at goal, Ramos and Benzema's composure from the spot proved critical.

Among the other goal types, the team scored seven off of set pieces (a 10% goal share), two immediately following a set piece (3%), and one own goal (>1%).

## Purchase Price vs Pre-2020/21 Season Market Value Comparision

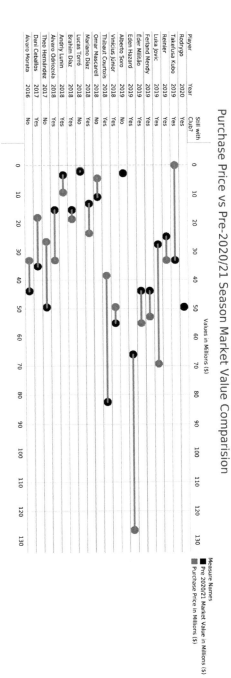

| Player | Year | Still with Club? |
|---|---|---|
| Rodrygo | 2020 | Yes |
| Takefusa Kubo | 2019 | Yes |
| Reinier | 2019 | Yes |
| Luka Jovic | 2019 | Yes |
| Ferland Mendy | 2019 | Yes |
| Eder Militão | 2019 | Yes |
| Eden Hazard | 2019 | Yes |
| Alberto Soro | 2019 | No |
| Vinícius Júnior | 2018 | Yes |
| Thibaut Courtois | 2018 | Yes |
| Omar Mascarell | 2018 | No |
| Mariano Díaz | 2018 | Yes |
| Lucas Torró | 2018 | No |
| Brahim Díaz | 2018 | Yes |
| Andriy Lunin | 2018 | Yes |
| Alvaro Odriozola | 2018 | Yes |
| Theo Hernández | 2017 | No |
| Dani Ceballos | 2017 | Yes |
| Alvaro Morata | 2016 | No |

Values in Millions ($)

Measure Names
- Pre 2020/21 Market Value in Millions ($)
- Purchase Price in Millions ($)

*Florentino Pérez's Clear Plan for the Future*

As the club moves on from their 2019/20 season, they do so with Florentino Pérez responsible for the transfer side of the business.

Looking at his transfers since 2016, the chart shows the club's purchase price of players held in relation to the pre-2020/21 market value in millions. These values come directly from Transfermarkt.

Keep in mind that player values have plummeted since the COVID-19 outbreak. With lower club revenues, the market price teams are willing to pay for players has dropped considerably. The impact on this chart in particular is that Pérez's purchases from the summer of 2019 have mostly dropped in value. That's a natural response to the financial market in the global game.

Looking near the bottom of the list, the players he's recruited have mostly surpassed their original purchase price. Granted, very few of those players are still under contract with the club, but that's less about raw talent identification than it is about fitting these mostly young talents into a side that's expected to compete for trebles each season. Patience is rarely an option in Madrid.

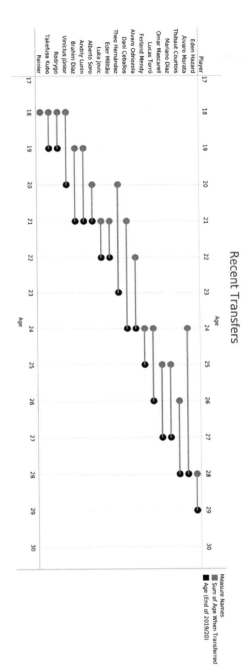

Recent Transfers

Speaking of young talents, the players' age at the time of the transfer shows what Pérez has in mind. The objective is to identify supremely talented youngsters that the club can mold into Real Madrid players. The younger players will generally have a year or two to prove their Real Madrid quality, either by immediately breaking into the lineup or showing that they're not far from it.

In the "Recent Transfers" chart, the left end of the line represents each player's age at the time of their arrival in Madrid. The right-endpoint indicates their age at the time of publication.

Beyond the young players, Pérez still has a little bit of that Galáctico mentality. After a considerable hiatus in the superstar transfer market, the purchases of Eden Hazard and Thibaut Courtois, both from Chelsea, served to bring in superstars for on and off the pitch purposes.

With no incoming transfers for the 2020/21 season and a number of players making their way out the door, this has all the signs of a sell-off before reinvestment. Financial limitations from the loss of fans in the stand, as well as the Santiago Bernabéu's remodeling, may hamstring the club in the near future, but there are a couple of young stars that would shine brightly in Madrid. Should Kylian Mbappe and Erling Håland arrive in the next couple of years, Pérez can check two boxes with one move, securing the new generation of Galáctico's who still happen to be in their early twenties.

But enough of the business side of things. Let's finish up with the people who carried the club to their 34th La Liga title.

*Benzema's Broad Shoulders*

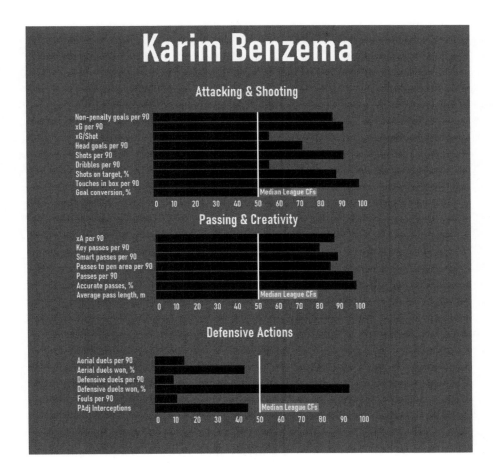

With 21 goals in 37 appearances, Benzema again ends the season as Real Madrid's leading goal scorer. With Vinícius Júnior and Marco Asensio leading the rest of the forwards in La Liga goals, finishing with three apiece, it's safe to say Benzema had a little help to produce goals. Kroos and Casemiro each had four, Modrić chipped in three, and then all other goal scorers either finished with one or two.

Well, all except one, but we'll get to him in a moment.

Returning our focus to Benzema, his 2019/20 season fits his Formula 1 description. In the attacking and shooting stats, as well as the passing and creativity sections of his player profile, Benzema doesn't rate below the 50th percentile in a single statistical category.

Perhaps the most phenomenal parts of his profile are rating in the 90th percentile for xG per 90 and rating in the 80th percentile or higher in nearly every passing and creativity stat.

Once again, Real Madrid's goal-scoring burden fell squarely on Benzema's broad shoulders. With Ronaldo at Juventus and Bale in and out of the lineup last season, then moving on loan to Tottenham for the 2020/21 campaign, the game's BBC is down to its final member.

As the primary goal-scorer, and really the only consistent threat in open play, on the team, Benzema's scoring exploits made him one of the first names on the team sheet. With 37 La Liga appearances, he led the team in the category.

Second place?

*Ramos' Career Year*

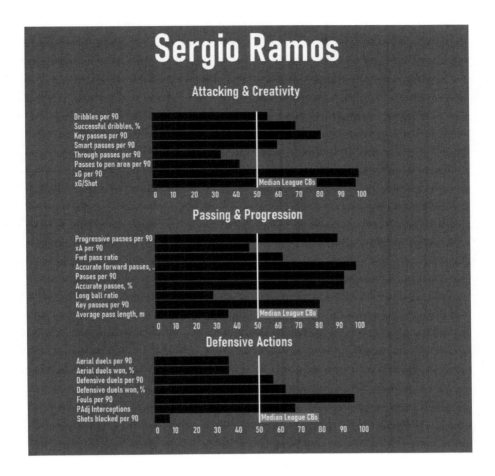

2nd in appearances was none other than the captain, Sergio Ramos. Take away the twice-annual suspensions and he would have equaled Benzema's mark.

Though he'll turn 34 in March of 2020, Ramos was still able to put together one of the best years of his career.

It was a season that saw him claim the record for most El Clásico appearances, making his 44th in March, equal the UEFA Champions League record for red cards with four, overtook Ronald Koeman as La Liga's all-time leading goal scorer among defenders, and setting his personal best with 11 La Liga goals in a season.

Real Madrid is simply a different team without their captain in the side. The Champions League performance against Manchester City, as well as some early 2020/21 matches, have shown just how critical he is to the team's success.

Whether he's scoring on penalty kicks or set pieces, beating the middle block with a long diagonal pass, or putting in a hard tackle, he's both a fiery performer and leader on the pitch.

His contract expires at the end of the 2020/21 season. The team does need to identify a successor, which they hopefully have in Eder Militão, but keeping the captain around for another couple of years would seem to benefit all parties involved. To centerbacks can play the high level well into their late 30s. Should the club offer Ramos a contract renewal, they'll secure the contract of a player who has defined the identity of the latest Real Madrid teams.

*Zidane's Legacy*

Finally, we have our man of the season, the great Zinedine Zidane, a club legend both on and off the field.

Twice he has rescued Real Madrid from the depths of despair, twice leading them back to the trophy platform.

Though the 2019/20 season marks the first time in his coaching career that he has not claimed the UEFA Champions League trophy, ripping the La Liga crown from Barcelona's head will certainly satiate the crowd.

**UEFA Champions League**
2015/16
2016/17
2017/18

**La Liga**
2016/17
2019/20

**Supercopa de España**
2017/18
2019/20

**FIFA Club World Cup**
2016/17
2017/18

**UEFA Super Cup**
2016/17
2017/18

**World's Best Club Coach**
2016/17
2017/18

As if he didn't win enough trophies as a player, Zizou continues to show the world that he is a winner. Season after season, he adds hardware to the halls of the Bernabéu. This season, he contributed both the La Liga title and the Supercopa de España trophy.

After a miserable 2018/19 season, Zidane has returned more than just the trophies. His presence goes beyond the tactics he brought to the team or his cerebral presence in the dugout.

Zinedine Zidane brings an identity.

After the club lost its way in 2018/19, Zidane figured out how to couple the talents and characteristics of his individual players with this revitalized image of the club.

Despite all the injuries, the mid-season slump, a 3-month layoff, and a painful Champions League exit, the enthusiasm, competitiveness, and passion of the players never waned. Even during the season's low points, the collective mentality brought on by Zizou was apparent to all.

He's more than just a coach. Zinedine Zidane is a standard-bearer.

Twice they've fallen, twice he's helped them back to their feet, returning the club to their lofty pedigree, the only standard he knows.

By restoring the club's identity, Zidane is revitalizing Real Madrid.

# Zinedine Zidane
## Attacking stats 2015/16

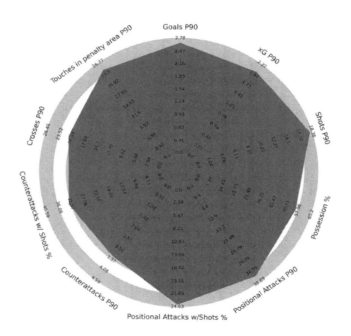

# Zinedine Zidane
## Defending stats 2015/16

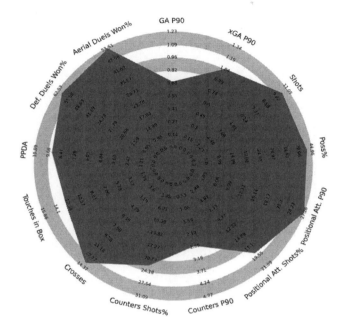

# Zinedine Zidane
## Attacking stats 2016/17

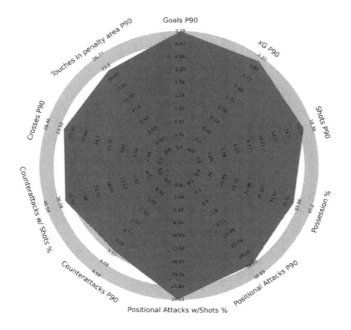

# Zinedine Zidane
## Defending stats 2016/17

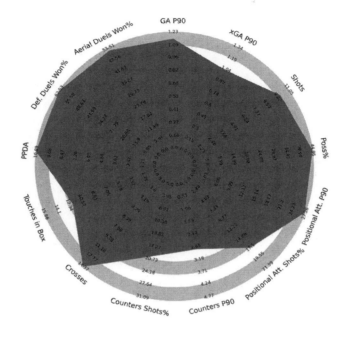

# Zinedine Zidane
## Attacking stats 2017/18

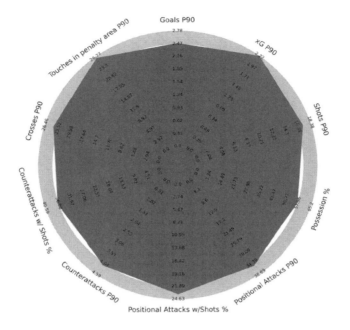

# Zinedine Zidane
## Defending stats 2017/18

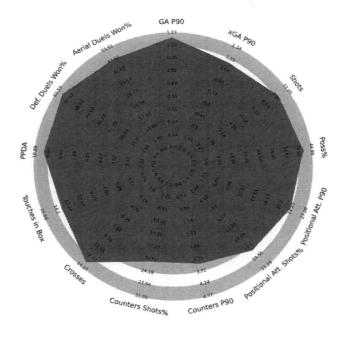

# Julen Lopetegui
## Attacking stats 2018
### August 19, 2018 - Ocotober 28, 2018

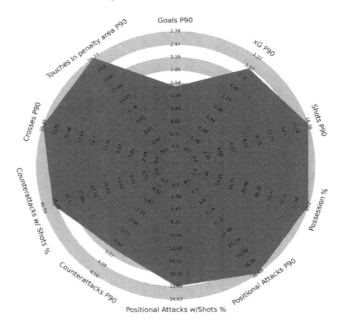

# Julen Lopetegui

## Defending stats 2018

### August 19, 2018 - Ocotober 28, 2018

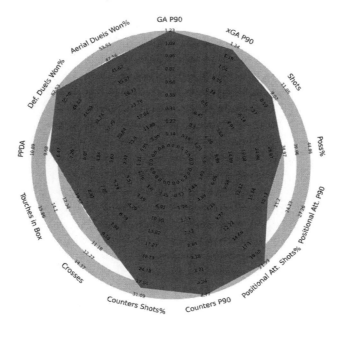

# Santiago Solari

## Attacking stats 2018/19

### November 3, 2018 - March 10, 2019

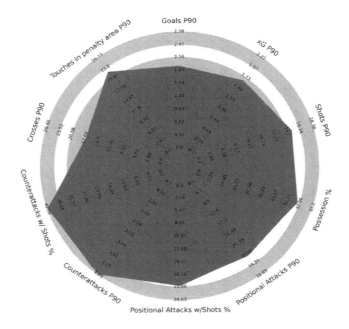

# Santiago Solari

## Defending stats 2018/19

### November 3, 2018 – March 10, 2019

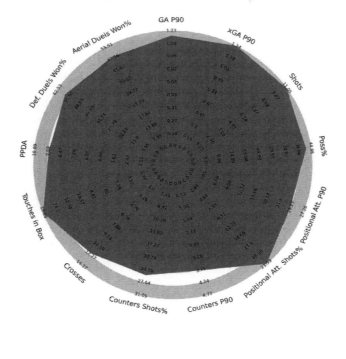

# Gareth Bale
## 2016/17

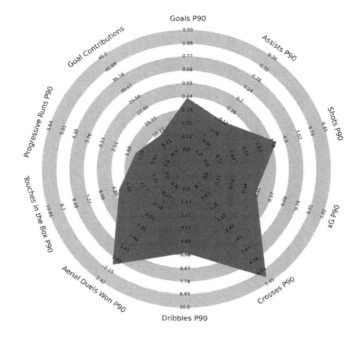

# Gareth Bale
## 2017/18

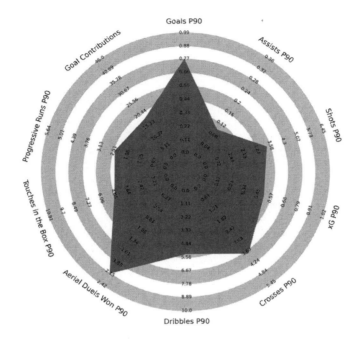

# Gareth Bale
## 2018/19

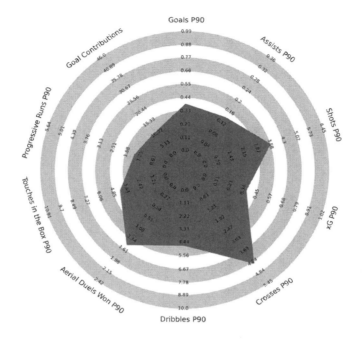

# Gareth Bale
## 2019/20

# Karim Benzema
## 2016/17

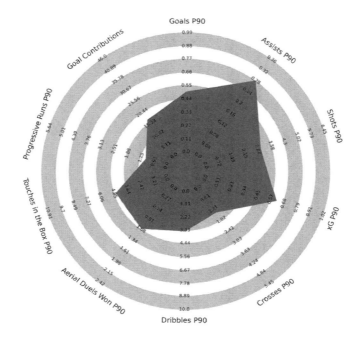

# Karim Benzema
## 2017/18

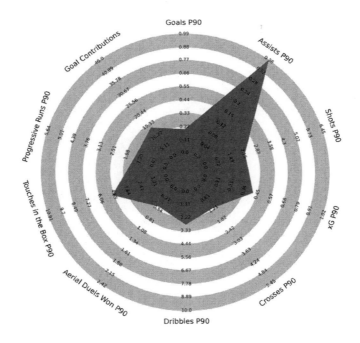

# Karim Benzema
## 2018/19

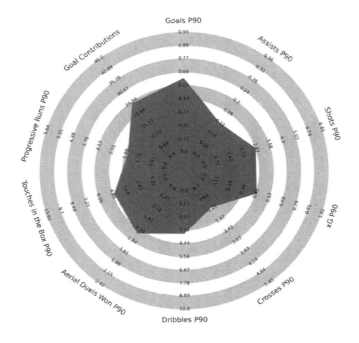

# Karim Benzema
## 2019/20

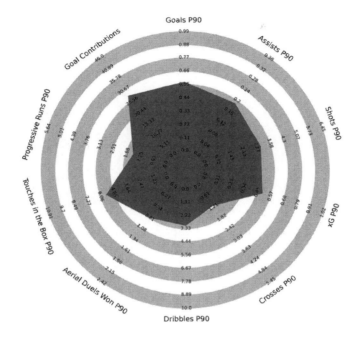

# Eden Hazard
## 2019/20

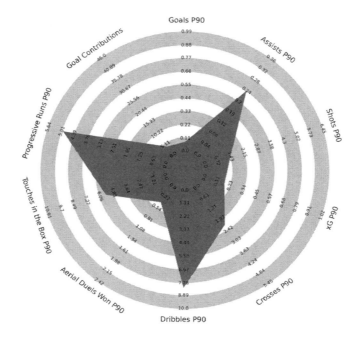

# Cristiano Ronaldo
## 2015/16

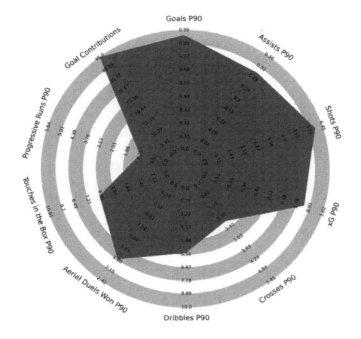

# Cristiano Ronaldo
## 2016/17

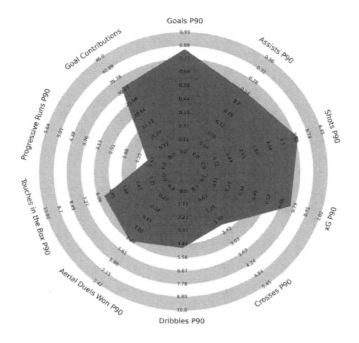

# Cristiano Ronaldo
## 2017/18

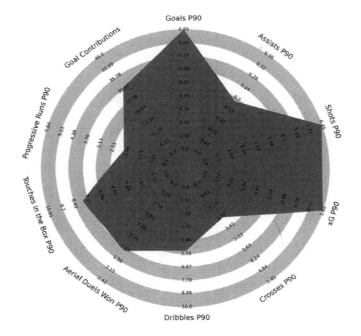

# Vinícius Júnior
## 2019/20

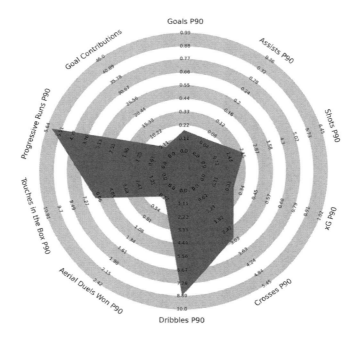

# Vinícius Júnior
## 2019/20

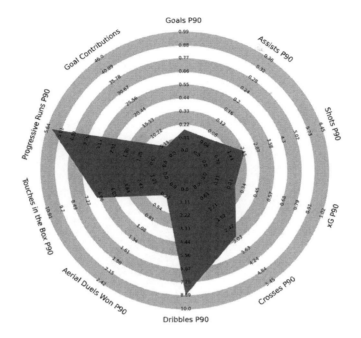

# Vinícius Júnior
## In Right Flank

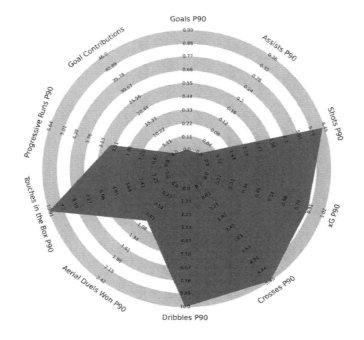

# Meet the Team

## Scott Martin

Scott is a senior analyst for Ronnie Dog Media (Total Football Analysis), youth soccer coach, and copywriter.

When life isn't consumed by soccer, he's spending time with his wife and two sons.

Revitalizing Real Madrid is his first book, but additional publications are in the works. To stay up to date on his latest work and sign up for his weekly newsletter delivering the week's best soccer content from around the web, subscribe to his website and follow him on social media.

Website: https://scottmartinmedia.com/
LinkedIn: https://www.linkedin.com/in/scottmartinamdg/
Twitter: https://twitter.com/CoachScottCopy
Facebook: https://www.facebook.com/ScottMartinSoccerAnalyst
Instagram: https://www.instagram.com/coachscottcopy/

## Sathish Prasad V.T

Sathish is a 20-year old pursuing his degree in computer science engineering and hails from Chennai, India. He excels in data analysis and aspires to work in a professional football club one day.

Currently working as an analyst at Ronnie Dog Media, he has acquired various knowledge required to enter the football industry with data visualization being his strongest areas and has also contributed visualizations to other books such as English Premier League - Preseason Prospectus 2020/21, Real Madrid - Preseason Prospectus 2010/21 and Barcelona - Preseason Prospectus 2020/21.

He also owns a separate Twitter account called Sideline Analysis(@TheTacticalEyes) with the sole purpose of analyzing Indian football, helping this component of football gain recognition and importance among fans in the country. When he's on a break, he spends most of the time playing football and listening to music.

Reach out to him at the following pages:
Website: https://vtsathishprasad.wixsite.com/sathishportfolio
Twitter: https://twitter.com/SathishPrasadVT
Linkedin: https://www.linkedin.com/in/sathish11/
Email: vtsathishprasad@gmail.com

## Jamie Brackpool

After finishing his education in Communications and Public Relations, Jamie pursued his dream of working in the football industry. As well as coaching full-time with RED Academy of Soccer, he works as a freelance designer.

He is currently working for Ronnie Dog Media designing their magazines and preseason prospectuses. Jamie is available for contract work in digital illustration and document layout design.

You can follow him on Twitter (@JamieBrackpool) where he enjoys cheering for - and moaning about - Manchester United. While he has stepped away from writing tactical analyses to focus on design, Jamie does still enjoy discussing and observing the tactical nuances of modern football.

Printed in Great Britain
by Amazon

27574201R00171